THE HEART TO MOVE FORWARD

THE HEART TO MOVE FORWARD

4 Steps to L.I.V.E. Again After the Loss of a Child

DYNITA T. WASHINGTON

Published by ELOHAI International Publishing & Media
P.O. Box 1883
Cypress, TX 77410
Website: www.elohaipublishing.com
Email: hello@elohaiintl.com

Cover Design: ELOHAI International Publishing & Media
Cover Photography: Snaps by Beauty-Full Jae

ISBN: 978-1-953535-23-8

Dedication

I dedicate this book to my firstborn son, Mark Allen Washington Jr., whose life paved the path to my destiny without me even knowing it. To my beloved husband, Mark Sr., who walked this journey alongside me and allowed me the time and space to complete this project. To my daughter, Naomi, who was so young for much of the timeframe this book is written about. Thank you for being my first proofreader. You are an incredible writer. To my two former foster sons, you know who you are: God placed you in our lives not just because you needed us but also because we needed you. All of you gave me a sense of purpose and a reason to get up every morning and move forward, even when I did not want to.

I also dedicate this book to my family members, who went down memory lane with me to help me remember and organize the many puzzle pieces of my story so I could produce this great work: Mom Paula, Mom Rita, Michael, George Jr., Veronica, Monica, Gregory, Darryl and Lila. Thank you to Fielding and my Dad, George Sr., for your words of encouragement during this assignment. Thank you for your prayers and support. It is because of all of you that I learned to live, laugh, and love.

Table of Contents

Part II—Recovering from Loss

Acknowledgements

Thank you, Sister Thomasina Williams (Ms. Tommie), of Abundant Life Fellowship Church, for your thoughtfulness and creativity. The special album you meticulously handcrafted with all the posts and responses on the CaringBridge website blog chronicling the last four-and-a-half months of our journey with Marky has been one of the best gifts ever. Words cannot express my deep appreciation for your forethought in doing this. Thank you for following God's lead and creating this album full of pictures, journal posts, and words of encouragement to help us remember how the Lord brought us through such a difficult time. This gift planted the seed for me to eventually write a book about this journey. I pulled it out fourteen years later and was reminded of the many people who had our backs. We love you.

Thank you to my in-laws, Darryl and Lila. When you came to visit us on Jan 2, 2021, you brought your video camcorder with some old home videos. Thank you for all the sweet memories you captured of our families over the years. Lila was often seen with the camcorder in hand to record the kids in all sorts of activities—dancing, singing, rough housing, playing in the hot tub, roller skating, birthday parties, and backyard barbecues. I watched the videos and was reminded of the painful, yet joyful, time we spent at A. I. duPont Hospital. We didn't know it then, but it was the last Christmas we would spend with our Marky. Your visit helped to confirm that this was the time for me to start writing again.

Thank you Pastor Joy Morgan of Restoration Station Christian Fellowship and Joy Morgan Ministries for living on purpose—motivating others to live up to their potential and reach their destiny. You planted and watered the seed so many years ago. And instead of giving up, you were patient with gentle reminders, offering many opportunities to learn how to write a book. Thank you for being the midwife, the coach, the cheerleader, and sometimes the correctional officer along the way. I am convinced that if you didn't live up to your calling, I would not have completed this project. I have a huge amount of gratitude for you and the Finish That Book Challenge cohort of authors for your encouragement and support.

Thank you, Natasha T. Watson and the ELOHAI International Publishing & Media team for your excellent teaching, coaching, and encouragement as you guided me through the writing and publishing process. I appreciate your patience when I asked so many questions and submitted multiple revisions. Thank you for helping me to see that this is not just a book, but the beginning of a movement. To God be the glory!

I give a special shout-out to my mother-in-love, Rita W. Bristol, who read through the entire book several times to proofread and help me find just the right scriptures to include. You read until your eyes were tired and burning. Thank you for your sacrifice. And thank you for capturing some very precious memories of Marky.

To my sister, Monica Sills, thank you for always having my back and using your anointed hands to create complimentary products for the book. I can always count on you for love and support.

To my "Sis", Jackie Cole, thank you for the adventurous photoshoot experience. The front cover and headshot photo credits belong to you. You and Monica make a great glam squad team.

Thank you to all my pastors who have taught me the Word of God, prayed for me, and provided the spiritual covering over me and my family throughout the years:

- Elder Honest Hawkins (deceased) and Elder Edward Wallace, former Pastors—St. Peter Primitive Baptist Church, Burlington, NJ
- Apostle Gilbert Coleman Jr., Overseer—Freedom Christian Bible Fellowship, Philadelphia, PA
- Lead Pastor Aubrey Fenton, Apostle Abraham Fenton, Rev. Dr. Eve Lynne Fenton (deceased), and Pastor Richard Minus—Abundant Life Fellowship Church, Edgewater Park, NJ
- Rev. Kevin Cain, Senior Pastor—Kingdom Evangelical Methodist Church, Morgantown, WV
- Dr. David Anderson, Senior Pastor—Bridgeway Community Church, Columbia, MD

Thank you to the healthcare workers who took great care of Marky and our family during our journey.

- Nemours/Alfred I. duPont Hospital for Children, Wilmington, DE
- Nemours duPont at Thomas Jefferson University Hospital, Philadelphia, PA
- Children's Hospital of Philadelphia
- Weisman Children's Rehabilitation Hospital, Marlton, NJ

Foreword

Dynita Washington is one of the strongest, faith-filled women I've ever met. I initially became acquainted with her through mutual church friends, but got to know her better when she and her family moved next door to my parents. It was during that time when I discovered she had a chronically ill son named Marky. At some point, her precious boy's illness became very serious, leading him to an extended stay in the hospital. During Marky's hospitalization, Dynita kept concerned friends and family up to date on his health status through a daily blog. I read the updates faithfully, in hopes that Marky's condition would improve so that he could return home to his family in a "happily ever after" ending.

Sadly, that is not how the story unfolded. Marky's health continued to worsen and he eventually went home to be with the Lord. Through the whole ordeal, I was both astounded and inspired by the strength and grace this dutiful mother conveyed in those daily blogs. While informing readers of the gravity of her six-year-old son's heart condition, she remained positive, upbeat, and hopeful. Facing what was undoubtedly the most difficult time of her life, it was evident through each journal entry, that her faith, hope, and spirituality served as anchors to keep her grounded and helped her to find peace and comfort through the roller-coaster ride of emotions.

I knew back then, as I read each daily blog, I was reading the makings of a book. It was my firm belief that this well-documented journey could be a source of inspiration to parents whose dreams for their children have been sidetracked by the diagnosis of a critical illness. So some time after Marky's passing, I asked Dynita to prayerfully consider turning her blog entries into a book. However, as to be expected, she first had to take the necessary time to process her pain and grief before sharing it with the world.

At the time of this writing, Marky would be celebrating his twenty-first birthday and Dynita is now ready to tell her heart-bending story of mothering a sick child in her highly anticipated book, *The Heart to Move Forward.* Dynita provides comfort, hope, and biblical counsel for parents of sick children or caretakers of anyone who is critically ill. I encourage you to open your heart as you turn every page of this book. Allow a mother who is well acquainted with your journey to minister to your pain and offer you hope in the God of comfort.

I am humbled and honored to have served as one of Dynita's midwives in birthing this book project. Through her insightful and candidly honest story, may you find purpose in your pain and beauty for ashes, just as Dynita has.

Pastor Joy Morgan

Restoration Station Christian Fellowship

Preface

I want to give a special acknowledgment to the parents who have lost a child through miscarriage, sudden death, or some other tragic circumstance. Oh, how my heart bleeds for you! I am aware your experience of losing a child is much different from my own. Although we are all grieving for our beloved children and feeling a huge void in our hearts, I recognize your pain may be at a different level because of the lack of time to get to know your child, or you had little or no opportunity to say goodbye. I wish we could turn back the hands of time to do so. You have my deepest sympathy.

I can only imagine the agony and disbelief felt when a loved one is taken away unexpectedly. The sorrow and grief must be even more intense than what I knew. Know that I am praying for you. I encourage you to seek the therapy needed to process your grief and allow yourself the necessary time to deal with your tremendous loss. I hope you will read this book and find some nuggets of truth that will lead you to the strength and courage to move forward. Even when it feels like a piece of our soul has died, I believe we can L.I.V.E. again after loss.

Introduction

The Heart to Move Forward is a compilation of real-life stories highlighting the beautiful journey my family had the privilege to travel. This memoir is meant for those who are traveling a similar path — a path filled with love, joy, faith, fear, and at times, grief. You will find emotional accounts of how my family managed to overcome the challenges that came with caring for a chronically ill child. We laughed, we cried, and we depended on God to get us through the tough times. When the doctors said they could do nothing more to help my child, we were heartbroken. As the story unfolds, you will see how we ultimately put our complete trust in God and were reminded that He still performs miracles today.

This book is for the parents and grandparents who walk the halls of doctors' offices and hospitals today, praying, hoping, believing, and sometimes pleading for a cure for your child's disease or injury. You may be wondering how their life will turn out. I pray you will experience the awesome joy and privilege of seeing your child healed and whole again so you can create and enjoy more memories with them. Don't stop praying and believing. There is hope because Jehovah-Rophe is our healer.

On the other hand, some of us witness our child going through a long, grueling illness filled with pain and difficulties. I share my story for those who must tear themselves away and leave their sick child at the hospital to return to work or back home to care for their other children and responsibilities. This book is for the ones who will eventually go home carrying only stuffed animals, doctors' notes, cards, and personal belongings that don't mean much anymore but may have to accept leaving the one that means the most in the hospital morgue with no more memories to be made. I tell my story to encourage the one who is in despair, the one who feels like this pain is too much to bear. You feel like you can't go on and just want to end it all. Well, I have some good news for you.

Although you may be faced with the harsh reality of losing your child, you can find the strength to move forward. As you read through my personal journey, I encourage you to listen out for lessons learned and the trail of wisdom I leave behind to help you persevere through your own journey. I pray as you read this book you will gain *The Heart to Move Forward* by focusing on the four steps to *L.I.V.E.*—**L**ove hard and laugh often, **I**nclude others on your journey, Check your **V**ital signs, and **E**ncourage somebody else. My prayer is that this narrative will give strength to the brokenhearted, hope for the hopeless, and purpose for your future. I am reminded of Jeremiah 29:11:

For I know the plans I have for you,
declares the Lord, plans to prosper you and
not to harm you, plans to give you hope and a future. (NIV)

How to Read This Book

This book is written from a Christian perspective, laced with Bible scriptures and short prayers to encourage you as you read. Each chapter will walk you through my personal journey, highlighting some of the joys and sorrows of parenthood. Follow along if you want to read the intricate details and see how God's orchestrated plan unfolds in my life.

There are two sections in the book. Part I will address how we managed our family while caring for our chronically sick child. Part II is the accounts of how I went through the stages of grief that eventually led me on the path to healing. In chapter eleven, I give you a peek into the window of how my daughter processed grief after losing her big brother. You can also head straight to chapter thirteen to learn the four steps to L.I.V.E. again after the loss of your child. In the final chapter of the book, I raise awareness of the need for organ and tissue donors and how we can play a role in saving others' lives.

For those of you who are looking for a guide to move forward, there are questions and prompts at the end of each chapter to help you navigate through your own journey of adversity, grief, and restoration. Whichever way you decide to engage with this narrative, I pray it will provide you the comfort, guidance, and courage to move forward so you can experience all that God has for you.

Are you ready to break free from your pain and LIVE?

PART I

Caring for a Chronically Ill Child

CHAPTER 1

Whose Report Do You Believe?

For unto us a child is born, unto us a son is given.
—Isaiah 9:6a (KJV)

"Honey! Cancel the cheesesteak," I shouted downstairs to Mark.

"Huh, what did you say?" Mark replied.

"I said cancel the cheesesteak order. I think my water just broke," I explained.

"What! Are you serious?" Mark exclaimed. I could hear my husband Mark was disappointed that he had to call Gaetano's Cheesesteaks to cancel the order he had placed moments ago. (Gaetano's was known for having the best, juiciest and biggest cheesesteaks in New Jersey, with hand-cut steak, dressed with fried onions and mushrooms served on specially made soft bread.)

We had just returned home from my weekly perinatal obstetrician visit in Philadelphia. It was around 5 p.m., and I was exhausted from the day's activities. Carrying around an additional thirty-five pounds of weight from the baby and all the extra that comes with it is not easy. My belly was huge and felt as hard as a basketball. Disappointed that the doctor was sending us back home instead of across the street to the hospital, I had succumbed to the reality of another night of waiting. The doctor said it wasn't time yet. I was getting close but had barely dilated a half centimeter. And technically, I had one more week to go before being declared full-term.

Mark grabbed the overnight bag out of the green Chevy Lumina and carried it back into the house. I went straight upstairs to the second floor of our yellow, four-bedroom Cape Cod house. I took off my shoes and climbed onto my bed to lay across the gold and burgundy comforter. As I tried to get myself comfortable with a pillow behind my back and the wedge pillow under my enormous belly so I could take a nap, I suddenly heard a loud pop and immediately felt water dripping between my legs. My eyes got big. Could this be it? Could this really be the onset of labor?

"Aw shucks," I said to myself as I scooched down to the bottom of the bed, grabbed the cordless telephone, and hurried into the bathroom. The water was escaping so fast. I pulled my fleece pants down and quickly sat on the toilet. However, as soon as I sat down, I could hear my mother, Paula, say, "Don't ever sit on the toilet when you're in labor." Ignoring that thought, I yelled for Mark's help to get me a towel and my purse so I could find the number to call my doctor. He brought them to me, and I immediately called the doctor's office. I was connected to the after-hours phone dispatcher. She took down my name and phone number and said she would contact the doctor to call me right back. In the meantime, I called my mother to tell her what was happening.

"Where are you," she asked.

"Sitting on the toilet," I replied. I knew what she was going to say next.

"Dynita, get off the toilet and get into the tub. You don't want the baby to slip out and fall into the toilet. It has happened to another woman before."

I was scared, so I listened to my mom and jumped into the tub. The water was draining out quickly. It was not a trickle or a stream.

It felt like a flood. By then, the doctor called me back on the phone, and I told him what was happening. He said I would be okay to sit on the toilet. Now I was conflicted between my mother, who raised me, and my doctor, who knew the details about my high-risk pregnancy. I thought about it for a second and decided I didn't want to sit in a tub of amniotic fluid. So I got up and returned to the toilet.

"Is that a faucet of water running?" The doctor asked.

I said, "No, that's my water breaking."

The doctor reminded me that I was carrying an abnormal level of amniotic fluid, so it was expected that the water break would be extensive. Since the contractions were still far apart and not painful, the doctor told me I could wait a while before coming to the hospital. Mark and I looked at each other, shaking our heads, "Oh no! We're not waiting around. We're heading to the hospital right away."

You see, this had not been a typical pregnancy. About nine weeks before this at my regular prenatal care checkup, the doctor detected the baby's heart rate was low, so he sent me directly to the hospital for fetal monitoring. We went to the emergency room at Rancocas Valley Hospital in Willingboro, New Jersey to get checked out. Within two hours, the baby's heart rate picked up and stabilized. We exhaled with a sigh of relief. Maybe all the baby needed to wake up was that jolt of apple juice I drank.

I was then taken to an examination room and prepared for an ultrasound. My husband is known for striking up conversations with strangers and making funny and sometimes awkward remarks to break the ice. At first, the ultrasound technician was light-hearted, laughing, and playing along with Mark's jokes. But then I noticed her demeanor changed. Her grin had gone solemn, and the cheery responses had abruptly ended. The silence grew uncomfortable. She left the room for a couple of minutes, leaving Mark and me to wonder what was going on. The OB-GYN emergency room doctor on call then came into the room, introduced herself, and recommended that we get another ultrasound by a perinatologist. They thought they saw something strange with the baby's digestive system. She told me that it's probably nothing, but I should be sure to drink lots more water to flush out my system. We scheduled the next ultrasound and were sent on our merry way. I said, "This encounter ended strangely, don't you think, Mark?" I could sense they were withholding more information, but they didn't want to be too hasty in communicating any specifics.

During this time in our lives, Mark and I were working full-time at the Wharton School of the University of Pennsylvania in West Philadelphia. We were both proud Penn alums, driven by our ambition, hoping to make a positive impact on society. We were counting on our Ivy League backgrounds to guarantee us gainful employment and business ventures, leading to upward mobility in life and ultimately success and happiness. Married for nearly four years, we had dreams of building an empire, having a family, and serving the Lord through our local church. We both came from humble beginnings. Mark and his four brothers grew up in a row house with their parents in a section of West Philadelphia known as "The Bottom." The nickname alone indicates that it was one of the poorer parts of the City of Brotherly Love. I, too, grew up in a working-class family in the New Yorkshire section of Burlington City in Southern New Jersey. Although my street was relatively quiet, lined with duplexes, housing mostly young families and a sprinkling of senior citizens, it was right around the corner from much of the drug and gang activity in our small town. My parents didn't allow me or my younger brother and sister to hang out in that section of town. It was off-limits, no questions asked.

Mark and I had come a long way from our modest starts in life. Although our parents didn't have a lot of money, they loved us and did everything they could to encourage us in our studies and to reach for something none of them had obtained—a college education. Mark and I met shortly after I graduated from Penn in 1995. He was working full time at Penn and taking night courses to finish his degree in business administration at the Wharton School. We fell in love and married a year later and set out to conquer the world together. When we found out I was pregnant, we were on top of the world. We were super excited to become parents, sharing the news with our relatives, church family, friends, and coworkers. We were happy as could be. Little did we know the trials that would await us in the coming months.

The Doctor's Call

That evening after the trip to the emergency room, my doctor from the Burlington County OB-GYN practice called me at about 6 p.m. I was startled by the call and thought right away that doctors rarely called after hours with good news. He began to tell me that the ultrasound detected some abnormalities with the baby. While more tests were needed to determine the depths of the abnormalities, they could see two large bubbles in the abdomen and a heart defect. It was a serious matter that could end with death in utero. I stared at the teal green carpet on our family room floor. I was stunned at the news. Or was I numb? To be honest, I don't know what I really felt. Maybe I was just afraid. The doctor referred us to a perinatologist for further testing and follow-up prenatal care. Mark and I immediately started praying for our baby. We called our parents to let them know, and they began praying for us as well.

The Diagnosis

My mom, Paula, accompanied us the next day to see the perinatologist at Rancocas Valley Hospital and offered us support. The doctor was a middle-aged Caucasian man wearing a white coat over his tall, thin build, with a seemingly bubbly demeanor. After initial introductions, he performed the ultrasound and tried to keep the conversation light and cheery. However, I was not in a cheery mood. I was concerned about the baby who was growing inside of me. During the ultrasound, they measured the baby's weight to be about three pounds. He finished the test and invited us to come into the conference room across the hall.

As we entered the conference room, I could see at least two additional medical professionals sitting around the rectangular table. We all sat down to hear the results of the test. Out of nowhere, we were blind-sided with a diagnosis that our baby was expected to have Down Syndrome because they could see two bubbles in the belly when there should only be one bubble. Furthermore, the heart didn't pass the four-valve cardiac test. Additionally, there was an increased amount of fluid around the baby. We were told these were the classic signs of Down Syndrome. The doctor and his team explained Down Syndrome is caused by chromosomal defects, not any environmental factors. So Mark and I could have done nothing to prevent this. It also had no bearing on having children in the future. Only an amniocentesis test could confirm it. This test requires a long, sharp needle to be injected into the abdomen to collect a small sample of the amniotic fluid. The thought of that evasive test scared me. Plus, there were risks to the baby to be considered.

The doctor went on and on about all the risks involved in continuing the pregnancy: going into labor early between thirty-two and thirty-six weeks, baby born with Down Syndrome, or some other kind of syndrome, fetal death in utero, or the baby could die shortly after birth. He went on to say that the baby would need a lot of medical attention if it made it through delivery and probably wouldn't have any chance of a thriving life. He even said he knew of a doctor in Wichita, Kansas who could terminate the pregnancy if we didn't want to take the pregnancy any further.

I couldn't believe what I was hearing. Just a few days ago, we were happy and excited about our little bundle of joy on the way, painting the nursery walls aqua blue with a decorative border featuring whales and other sea life creatures. The baby was very active, especially at night, making it hard to sleep. But in this moment, I was overcome with all sorts of emotions and began to sob in the conference room. Frankly, I was at a loss for words, but my husband spoke up right away, expressing that we were not receiving that recommendation to terminate the pregnancy and that he would write a letter to the doctor declaring the victory of the baby not being born with Down Syndrome. Mark and I never even considered abortion. How dare they tell us that there was no hope for our child? We were going to continue with the pregnancy and trust God for the direction in which He would take our lives. We believed in the power of prayer, and we saw God work healing miracles before, so we began praying for a miracle.

We left the conference room and exited out of the nearest door into the afternoon sunlight. I was feeling down in my spirit as we walked toward our cars in the sparse parking lot. Before my mom got into her car, she did the one thing that had carried her through tough times, the tried-and-true practice that carried her mother and her mother's mother through times of adversity—she prayed. My mom grabbed our hands and started lifting up a word of prayer for us and for her grandchild who was to come. I thank God for a praying mother, who not only tells you she's going to pray for you but stops whatever she's doing and starts praying right then. Even until this day, every time her adult children say we are traveling a long distance, have a job interview, or if someone in our house is sick, she sends a prayer text to cover us right away. That's how I learned to pray—watching my mom pray and seeing the fruit of her prayers. I've been covered in prayer all my life, but this time was different. I was so disturbed by the medical report that I could barely utter a prayer for myself. So I was truly dependent on my mother's prayers and that of others. Lord, let your will be done.

My mom had informed her pastor at St. Peter Primitive Baptist Church about the need for prayer for her unborn grandchild. She called me on a Sunday and asked if it was alright for her and the ministers to stop by my house that evening to pray with me. I said, "Yes, of course." Not only did Elder Maurice Talley come, but Evangelist Louise Jackson and her husband, Deacon Ezell Jackson, arrived at our home. We welcomed them inside and invited them to have a seat. However, I distinctly remember Pastor Talley said, "We didn't come to stay long or to socialize. We came to do the will of the Lord." As they remained standing in my family room, I shared the doctor's report about the baby. Mark pushed the coffee table on wheels off to the side of the room. Pastor Talley instructed Evangelist Jackson and my mom to lay hands on my belly, and he and the Deacon laid hands on Evangelist Jackson. My husband was behind me praying with his hands on my shoulders. With my hands lifted up, Pastor Talley offered up a powerful prayer of healing for our baby, strength for the journey, and divine direction for our lives. We appreciated that they would take time out of their busy schedules to come pray with us. As they left, we felt uplifted and hopeful that our baby would be alright.

Spiritual Battle

I opened my journal, where I kept weekly logs of the sermon notes from church. Our prophetic pastor had just preached from 1 Samuel 17. It is the account of when David, a young shepherd boy, meets up with the war hero Goliath. Everyone assumed that David would be killed by Goliath's sword because of Goliath's enormous size and experience in battle. However, David had a secret weapon. Along with his five smooth rocks and a sling, he had the Holy Spirit with him. By using an extraordinary strategy, David defied the odds and slayed the giant. It was a miracle David won that battle without a sword and shield. He had God on his side. The pastor went on to say, "God prepares you for every crisis that comes your way." I was reminded that this battle belonged to the Lord. So let God fight the battle. He may change hearts, remove persons, or turn around the circumstances.

In my journal, I wrote:

[As of yesterday, 3/17/2000], I came face-to-face with the Goliath in my life, a doctor's diagnosis of a seriously ill unborn child, but I declared this sickness would be defeated just as David defeated Goliath. I needed to fortify my strength for this battle, prepare for the spiritual warfare that I faced. I wrote a list of songs to encourage myself and to claim the victory over my life. The song list included "I'm so Glad Jesus Lifted Me," "Victory is Mine," "I am the God that Healeth Thee," "I'm Looking for a Miracle," "My Help Cometh From The Lord," "In Everything Give Him Thanks," and "When I Think of the Goodness of Jesus." While I was in my kitchen washing the dishes and wiping down the countertops, I was singing and praying. I had my own praise fellowship with God and my unborn baby. This helped to build up my courage and faith in God. Instead of focusing on the doctor's report, I focused on the promises of God. I did not ignore the doctor's report because I acknowledge they are highly skilled and trained to detect and treat sickness and disease. But you have to be careful because they will paint a picture of doom and gloom for your life. In order to keep my heart uplifted with

hope, I drew a line in the sand. I was not going to dwell on the negative possibilities. I was determined to focus on the positive possibilities. Whose report do you believe? We shall believe the report of the Lord.

I also read Mark 11:23-26:

"Truly I tell you, if anyone says to the mountain 'Go throw yourself into the sea' and does not doubt in their heart but believes that what they say will happen, it will be done for them. Therefore, I tell you, whatever you ask for in prayer, believe that you have received it, and it will be yours. And when you stand praying, if you hold anything against anyone, forgive them, so that your father in heaven may forgive you your sins." (NIV)

I needed to do the spiritual preparation by aligning myself with the Word of God. I needed to forgive some people in my life. I listed eleven people who had wronged me, dating back to my childhood. I knew the negative feelings I harbored were taking up space in my heart, and I needed to release them. I didn't need to have a conversation with them or tell them I forgave them. Some of them were probably unaware or had forgotten about the offense anyway. I decided to pray for God's help to forgive each one of them. After I released them, then I asked God to forgive me of my sins. I didn't leave any stone unturned. I was ready for this spiritual battle.

Is It a Boy or a Girl?

Mark and I agreed it was time to head to the hospital. He grabbed some large plastic trash bags to line the seats of our brown 1983 Toyota Corolla stick shift. I grabbed the packet of papers off the nightstand before heading downstairs to leave for the hospital. It was a list of scriptures given to me by a dear elderly lady from our church.

I had been reciting these scriptures daily ever since she gave them to me when I was about thirty-two weeks pregnant, and I made sure I had them as a source of encouragement and hope for a healthy baby.

It was now the middle of rush hour, and it typically took about forty-five minutes to get into downtown Philly from Willingboro. We pulled up to the emergency entrance at Thomas Jefferson University Hospital in Center City. Medical personnel met me at the front entrance with a wheelchair. Mark gave me a kiss before I was wheeled off into the labor and delivery ward of the hospital. And he hastily went to find a parking garage nearby. Finding a parking space in the city is almost always a challenge, so I figured I wouldn't see him for a while. We passed through several hallways before reaching the maternity and delivery ward. I was checked in at the front desk and soon placed in a tiny room with a bed and a single chair. My eyes were wandering around. This didn't look like a delivery room to me—more like a holding room. I was in a small room without windows, but I remember it being nicely decorated with a floral design. I changed out of my clothes and into a hospital gown.

By now, I was having contractions, but strangely they were not painful. I was still smiling and excited this day had finally come. Soon my mom, Paula; Mark's mom, Rita; and my younger sister, Monica had arrived at the hospital to be with us and see the baby born. We chose to keep the sex of the baby a surprise, so the baby was referred to as Baby Washington.

The night shift had just begun at 7 p.m., and with all the anticipated problems that the prenatal tests presented, the medical staff did not really want me to deliver the baby overnight. Their concern was never voiced, but I could read between the lines. The labor pains were starting to come, although spread out. By that time, Mark had parked the car and found me in that huge hospital. Hopefully, he had found some dinner to eat before joining me in the hospital room because I knew he was definitely hungry. I asked for a pain reliever. Much to my surprise, the medical personnel said, "No problem." The anesthesiologist gave me some medicine to take the edge off. I felt so good. I couldn't eat anything but ice chips, but that was ok. Whatever sacrifices I needed to make for the smooth delivery was okay with me. They checked my cervix, and I was only one centimeter dilated. Now all the women who have had babies or have been in a delivery room know that this is only the beginning. The doctors won't even consider giving you an epidural at that time. Well, I only asked for the epidural one time, and *bingo*, they said, "Good idea" and rolled in the medication cart and equipment to get it started. I was like, "Wow, this is easy. What are all these other women complaining about?" But little did I know, they wanted to slow down the progress of the delivery because the night shift staff were not fully equipped to handle this fragile baby if delivered at that time.

My sister, Monica, was there holding me still while they put the epidural in my back. Funny how things happen. Just nine months prior, the tables were turned. I was holding Monica still while she was given the epidural. She was delivering her daughter, Alexis. And that was the first time I had ever been inside of a delivery room. After I saw everything that happened, I was spooked and told them I wasn't ready to have any kids. However, there I was in the delivery room, trying to keep still so the epidural could be placed correctly. I was eventually moved to a larger delivery room. My mom and mother-in-law were there too. Initially, we were told that only three people could be in the delivery room with me, but we insisted that they bring in an extra recliner chair. This was my support team, and each played a significant role. They had walked closely with us through the pregnancy, praying with us and for us. They took turns going to the various doctor appointments. Each of them wanted to be there to see the manifestations of their prayers.

Eventually, I was comfortable enough and went to sleep to get some rest, but around 3:30 a.m. I awoke abruptly and had a sudden strong urge. "Monica, Monica." I woke up my sister and told her, "Feels like I need to use the bathroom. Please get me a bed pan."

Monica smiled with a giggle and said, "No, that means it's time. That's the feeling that you want to push." She quickly got the nurse.

The nurse told me, "No, no, no, no, no! Whatever you do, *don't push*. The doctor isn't here yet."

Can you believe I was told to wait until 7 a.m. when the morning shift was on duty? Was she really serious? Did she think I could hold it? I had the same feeling when you have to go to the bathroom (number two) really bad. You can only hold it for so long. My mom could see that the medical residents and staff were scrambling around trying to get things set up. They were looking nervous. I finally told the nurse to call everyone and tell them that their shift was starting earlier and they needed to come right away. Finally, after about three hours of hard labor pains, they allowed me to officially push. The resident doctor was young and looked so nervous. Jefferson Hospital is a "teaching hospital," so my room was flooded with lots of residents and interns. It seemed like fifteen or so of them surrounded my bed. Even though I am generally a private person, I didn't really care who was watching because I needed to deliver this baby right away. I don't really remember how long I was pushing, probably about thirty minutes, and with the help of forceps, our baby boy was born at 6:56 a.m. We had already decided if the baby was a boy, we would name him Mark Jr. and nickname him Marky. I gave him a quick kiss before they rushed him off to the neonatal unit to examine him. My baby was finally here. He was alive, breathing on his own. He had ten toes and ten fingers. He had a head full of hair, hence the heartburn during pregnancy. He looked good to me on the outside, but only God knew what was going on inside his little body.

I was eventually taken to my room to recover, still numb, sore, and exhausted. My husband unplugged the phone so I could get some sleep. Then something scary happened. I couldn't remember what my baby boy looked like. I had only seen him for a minute or so. And I couldn't remember his face. Was I a bad mother? I cried. So my husband went to the Neonatal Intensive Care Unit (NICU) and a nurse took a Polaroid picture of Marky to send to me. Ah, that's better. At least now I know who I should be thinking of while I was recuperating and he was undergoing all sorts of tests in the building next door to me; it felt like we were miles apart. I asked Mark to go check on our baby while I rested. I wanted him to be nearby in case there were any sudden changes in Marky's status. I closed my eyes and began to thank the Lord for his goodness. The Lord had answered our prayers. I had made it to thirty-nine weeks in my pregnancy, and our baby boy was born alive. If I had listened to that doctor who offered the opportunity of an abortion, I would have destroyed any possibilities of my son's first breaths and the opportunity for God to work a miracle. Instead, I chose to:

Trust in the Lord with all your heart, and lean not on your own understanding. In all your ways acknowledge Him and He shall direct your paths.
—Proverbs 3:5-6 (NKJV)

Challenge:

1. Have you received a bad diagnosis or medical report? If so, what was the diagnosis?

2. Are you focused more on that diagnosis, or are you putting your faith in God?

Prayer Focus: Father God, I thank You for my doctors and the expertise in their field. I pray that You give my doctor the wisdom and knowledge on how to best provide treatment. I recognize that sometimes You choose to heal our bodies with the help of the doctor. And other times, You are able to perform a miracle. I thank You for my healing however you deliver it.

CHAPTER 2

Fearfully and Wonderfully Made

I praise You because I am fearfully and wonderfully made;
Your works are wonderful, I know that full well.
— Psalm 139: 14 (NIV)

Marky surprised all the medical professionals on his case when he arrived without any sign of Down Syndrome. I would have loved him just the same, even if Down Syndrome was confirmed. I know that God never makes a mistake, and he provides us the resources and the grace to manage the situations we find ourselves in. God doesn't give us what we can handle. God helps us handle what we are given.

Marky was rushed out of the delivery room to the NICU for immediate examination of his heart and lungs. As a precautionary measure, Marky was initially intubated. However, the doctor quickly realized his lungs were fully developed and he could breathe on his own, so they extubated him to room air. The cardiologist, Dr. Paul Anisman, from the Nemours/Alfred I. duPont Hospital for Children was there to evaluate Marky's heart with an echocardiogram, which is a type of ultrasound of the heart. It is a non-evasive test that gives the doctors a detailed view of the cardiac function.

The test confirmed Marky had a complex congenital heart defect with a single atrium. The wall between the two ventricles in a normal heart never formed in Marky's heart. It was called Hypoplastic Left Heart Syndrome (HLHS) with a double outlet right ventricle. Although this anomaly was very serious, his heart was stable at birth. The cardiologist recommended Marky have heart surgery at six months old. At this point, the gastro intestinal tract defect took precedence.

The most immediate need was to address the double bubble, or duodenal atresia, in his abdomen. Duodenal atresia is the congenital absence or complete closure of a portion of the lumen of the duodenum, which is the first part of the small intestines. It causes increased levels of amniotic fluid during pregnancy (polyhydramnios) and intestinal obstruction in newborn babies (Wikipedia).

We prayed and interceded for our child to be able to handle this surgery. His body seemed so fragile, although he weighed in at five pounds ten ounces and 19 ½ inches long at birth. He was considered the heavyweight in the NICU, compared to all the other precious babies who were born prematurely and underdeveloped. So at least he had size on his side.

Although Marky was kept in the NICU, there were no residential facilities where parents could stay. Mark commuted back and forth each day to the hospital. My heart ached at the thought of leaving my child at the hospital while he was still in such a vulnerable state. He couldn't eat by mouth until after he had the surgery.

Before Marky was born, I researched the benefits of breastfeeding, especially when the child has health issues. It was the least I could do for my child, given I'd be unable to handle and care for him during the early days of his life. The maternity nurse showed me how to pump milk using an electric breast pump provided by the hospital. I started pumping milk and storing it in the freezer in the NICU as soon as I was able to. Each mother had to be sure to label their bags with their baby's name. Although Marky couldn't drink yet, the breast milk could be stored in the freezer for up to six months, so I had confidence he'd get to it eventually.

The hospital social worker arranged for Mark and me to stay in a one-bedroom apartment a block away from the hospital for a few days while Marky underwent surgery. It was a residence hall for the graduate students at Thomas Jefferson University. We were grateful for the accommodations and transitioned to the apartment as soon as I was discharged from the hospital [on May 25, 2000]. I recuperated there and visited Marky in the NICU throughout the day and during evening visiting hours. We lived on the hospital cafeteria meals and the food truck cuisine that lined the curbs of 11th and Walnut Streets in Philly. One day, Mom Rita brought us plates from Dawn's Memorial Day barbecue, including her famous baked beans with ground beef. We especially enjoyed the homemade food.

Mark and I continued praying for our son. We were careful to use positive words and to speak the word of faith over our lives. Just when fear and anxiety might try to creep its way into my thoughts, I would get a phone call from someone. One in particular was a call from Deacon Sylvester Roland from my home church, St. Peter Primitive Baptist Church in Burlington, NJ. He was the deacon assigned to me as a young girl, ever since I was baptized and became an official member of the church at the age of eight. He and his lovely wife, Deaconess Juanita Roland, watched me grow up physically and spiritually and offered me sound advice as I journeyed through my adolescence, teen, and college years. They attended our wedding ceremony and bid us well wishes as Mark and I started our life together. Now at twenty-seven years old, a new mother facing a critical time in my life, I heard the voice of Deacon Roland on the other end of the phone line. He offered congratulations on the birth of our baby boy. The conversation was brief, but consoling; as he gave encouraging words based on the holy Scriptures to uplift our hearts, he let us know that he and his wife were praying for us and assured us that God would be with us every step of the way. Even though I was no longer a member of St. Peter Church, we maintained close ties with them over the years.

God sent many reminders to us to keep our eyes on him and his promises. We had to walk by faith and not by sight (2 Corinthians 5:7). Through emails, phone calls, greeting cards, visits, balloons, and flowers, we learned to keep our heads held high in the midst of what really was a crisis of belief.

First Surgery

At three days old, Marky underwent his first operation. Mark and I were given special permission to visit Marky early that morning before visiting hours began and to briefly meet with the doctor to hear once again about the surgical plan. We prayed for him and gently touched his hand and arm as he rested under the baby warmer and soft light, letting him know we were standing right by his side. Once again putting our trust and faith in God to see him over another hurdle, we declared healing and victory for our son.

The surgeons repaired the duodenal obstruction. Other abnormalities were confirmed while he was on the operating table. Marky had situs inversus, which is a genetic condition in which the organs in the chest and abdomen are positioned in a mirror image from their normal positions. For example, the stomach appeared to be on the right as opposed to the left, and the duodenum was on the left side. The doctor identified multiple spleens but could not yet determine if any of them were functional. Although the appendix looked healthy, they decided to remove it now so it wouldn't cause any problems or confusion later in his already complex anatomy. While they had him under sedation, they also performed the circumcision at our request.

We thanked God the surgery was a success. Marky tolerated it well. He was now on the path to getting daily feedings through the nasogastric tube (NG tube), which was inserted through the nose into his stomach during the operation. Although he could not eat by mouth yet, the tube feedings helped provide the nutrition so his body could heal from the surgery and grow. In the meantime, I continued to store breast milk in the freezer in the Mother's Room, which was a separate small room within the NICU. There were several rocking chairs, nursing pillows, electric breast pumps, a refrigerator, a freezer, a sink, and a bathroom. The walls were lined with various posters, some informational with lactation instructions; others were inspirational to help decrease the anxiety and fears of the mothers. Surely anyone whose baby had to be cared for in the NICU had special needs, which typically led to angst and uneasiness. This room was intentionally decorated to be warm, inviting, and encouraging.

Two weeks after the surgery, Marky was introduced to bottle feedings. Mark and I took turns holding him in the rocking chair right next to the baby crib. I was elated to finally be able to cradle him in my arms and feed him. His eyes looked up at me as if he was in awe of his mommy. I would softly sing lullabies to him and tell him how much I loved him. I assured him that he would be alright. Saddened each night when I had to leave him at the hospital to go home, I prayed God would continue to watch over our little Marky. It was getting difficult. I longed to have my baby boy close by me all the time. I spent the evenings pumping breast milk while looking at a few beautiful photos we captured of him and returning phone calls from concerned family and friends. I could not drive yet, so I relied on Mark and others to drive me to Philly daily. It was convenient for Mark to make hospital visits after work since he worked at Penn.

He would grab dinner in the cafeteria and then come and spend a couple of hours in the NICU getting to know his namesake. When the final call for the end of visiting hours were announced by 7:55 p.m., we were saying our goodbyes to Marky and showering him with as many hugs and kisses as we could. Then I gathered my things and we journeyed through the long hallways to the parking garage for the lonely drive home. Yes, we had each other and we loved each other, but leaving our precious gift at the hospital each night left a void in our hearts. We clung to God and to each other during this difficult period.

Marky improved week by week. The Lactation Specialist met with Marky and me privately in the Mother's Room to teach me how to breastfeed him. It took many tries and a big dose of patience before Marky figured out how to latch on and feed himself. We had one small problem though. He kept falling asleep before finishing a full feeding. So it took some time for him to work up to full feedings before he could go home with us. I tickled his feet or his side to arouse him when I saw his eyes waning. This helped keep him awake longer, so he had fuller feedings. Occasionally, Mark would join me in the Mother's Room when it was empty. He took pride in talking with Marky while he ate and then would put him on his shoulder to burp him. Mark seemed to have a special knack for burping Marky on cue. I didn't always have that success and patted him on the back for what seemed like forever before giving up and hoping that he already burped before laying him down for a nap. As we got closer to Marky's release, the nurses would allow us to change his diapers and give him baths.

Father's Day... Oh Happy Day

On Father's Day, I was happy to wake up and see my husband beaming with pride as he read the first Father's Day greeting card he would receive that day. One year ago, Mark was not so happy. I can remember we were getting out of the car, dressed in our Sunday's best, giving ourselves the once-over in the car reflection to make sure our outfits laid just right. I noticed Mark's eyebrow slightly furrowed, indicating something was wrong. I couldn't understand why Mark wasn't in a good mood.

"What's bothering you, Honey?" I asked.

"I'm not happy today," he said.

"Why not?" I probed.

"Because I'm not a father yet. I want to be a father," he explained.

I realized that going to church and celebrating the fathers was particularly hurtful. Mark's father passed away long ago when Mark was only fifteen years old. And his goal of becoming a father had not become a reality yet. I could hear the pain in his voice, and I knew it confirmed that it was time to start a new chapter in our marriage. I had just graduated with my master's degree from Penn's Graduate School of Education in May. So there was no better time than now to start trying. As we made our way through the parking lot at Abundant Life Fellowship Church, I put my hand on his shoulder and said, "Next year, you will be a father." I sealed it with a kiss and a smile. He graciously agreed to my promise, and we entered the church for worship. And now at last, his dream of becoming a father had come true.

After church, we grabbed a quick bite to eat and went to the hospital to visit Marky. When we walked into the nursery, we found a colorful display with Father's Day greetings. It was adorned with Marky's foot and handprints and laminated as a keepsake to mark the celebration of fatherhood. This must have taken some extra effort from the nurse, because we noticed Marky's feet were turned inward and his hands were cupped closed and stiff at birth. We had to slowly stretch and massage his hands and fingers over time so they could take on a more natural form. But no matter what, this handmade Father's Day card was beautiful and touched his dad's heart. Mark picked up his son out of the crib and held him close to relish in the moment.

The nurses on duty made sure every father who walked through those doors on that day was acknowledged and made to feel special. Fathers play an important role in their children's lives. Besides helping with washing baby bottles and changing diapers, a father aspires to be a stabilizing presence for their children. A father wants to provide for his children by doing whatever is necessary to put a roof over their heads, clothes on their backs, and food on the table. And in our case, making sure we had adequate medical insurance, transportation to get back and forth to multiple doctor appointments, and providing for whatever special needs Marky had. Mark wanted to be the dad who witnessed every stage of growth, teach life lessons, and model being a provider for his family. He was certainly ready for this challenge.

Ready to Go Home

Three days before Marky was discharged from the hospital, he reached the milestone of full feedings. Since Marky gained weight throughout his hospital stay, the medical care team felt comfortable stopping the tube feedings and removed the NG tube. Mark and I took an infant CPR class at the hospital and read through the various material we were given to make sure we were ready to take Marky home. On June 27, Mom Rita, and her friend drove me to the hospital. But this time was a little different because I brought the car seat. Upon arrival, a hospital staff person came out to the car in the parking loop to make sure the car seat was installed correctly and reviewed how I was to have the baby strapped in rear-facing. Then we entered the hospital and took the elevator to the eighth floor to the NICU. Smiling from ear to ear, I greeted the nurses one by one to thank them for taking care of Marky for the past thirty-six days. We had grown to be a family in the NICU. We received final instructions about Marky's care. Then I got him dressed, strapped him safely in the carrier, and walked out of the double doors of the NICU. We were happy to leave that chapter behind us.

While riding in the elevator, Mom Rita said, "Look at him, turning his head and looking up at me!" Her second grandchild was following her voice and trying to make out who was so excited to see him. I carried him out to the car, buckled the car seat in securely, and sat in the back seat with him all the way home. I could barely take my eyes off him. Finally, I could bring my baby home and take care of him.

In 2017, late-night TV host Jimmy Kimmel and his wife, Molly, had a son named Billy. He was diagnosed with a congenital heart defect called Tetralogy of Fallot with pulmonary atresia just three hours after he was born. You can imagine Jimmy and Molly were terrified at this unexpected news, but they relied on their family's strength and their faith in God to help their baby get the treatment needed to recover. Baby Billy endured two open-heart surgeries as an infant. They were successful surgeries, and they were both elated to have Billy at home, living [a normal] life.

The next year, Jimmy opened up in *O*, The Oprah Magazine, saying that he and his wife feared getting too close to Billy.

> *"There were secrets we kept from each other that we revealed only after the second surgery," he said. "The biggest one was that I think subconsciously, we didn't want to get too close to the baby because we didn't know what was going to happen."*

I appreciated Jimmy's honesty and transparency. I could certainly understand why Jimmy and Molly felt that way. It pained me to hear that they suffered in silence with the dread of uncertainty. It is simply human nature to try to protect ourselves from the possibility of hurt and pain. When we sense danger, our initial reaction is to be afraid and run the other way. Unlike me, they didn't have a warning that their child would have a heart defect. Therefore, they were completely caught off guard with no time for preparation. This happens to many parents.

According to the Centers for Disease Control and Prevention (CDC) birth defects affect one in every thirty-three babies (about three percent of all babies) born in the United States each year. Birth defects are the leading cause of infant deaths, accounting for twenty percent of all infant deaths. Congenital heart defects (CHDs) affect nearly one percent—or about 40,000—births per year in the United States. Congenital heart defects are the most common types of birth defects, and fortunately, babies born with these conditions are living longer and healthier lives. Marky and Billy both had critical CHDs because they were required to have surgery or other procedures within the first year of life.

I am not here to judge if Jimmy and Molly's fear of getting close to their infant was right or wrong. Many of us who hear our child's diagnosis of a life-threatening illness are naturally afraid. Number one, we generally don't know much, if any, details about the illness. What we don't know can be scary. However, after getting past the initial shock of the news, we can take the time to research the illness and the possible treatments. Since Mark and I had about two months to process the pre-diagnosis of our unborn child, we made a conscious decision not to allow this news to change our direction. We were committed to having our child, and we even decided to name our child after my husband if he was a boy. Some would say that was bold and foolish. I say it is a statement of our faith in God and trust in His Word.

And we know that in all things God
works for the good of those who love him,
who have been called according to his purpose.
—Romans 8:28 (NIV)

CHALLENGE:

1. What problem do you face today that you don't know how to handle?

2. What do you need to trust God for today?

PRAYER FOCUS: Loving God, I thank You that one day You'll wipe every tear from my eyes because You're greater than every heartache or difficulty I'll ever face. Help me to trust You with my life.

CHAPTER 3

To Work or Not to Work—That Is the Question

*"Trust in the Lord with all your heart
and lean not on your own understanding;
in all your ways acknowledge Him, and He shall direct your path."
—Proverbs 3:5, 6 (NKJV)*

After Marky came home from the hospital, my whole world revolved around him. He brought so much joy to our lives. The first couple of months were a bit painful though, while we tried to get his sleeping schedule on track. While he was in the hospital, he was used to the lights on 24/7, and a nurse was always on duty to meet his every need. But here at home, I had to coax him into our home sleep schedule. On many nights I was awake in the wee hours of the morning, changing diapers, feeding him, and rocking him back to sleep. He would sleep for about an hour and then awake, crying at the top of his lungs. I couldn't just let him cry forever. It's a good thing I had some pillows reupholstered for an old rocking chair we had in the nursery because I anticipated spending lots of time in that chair cradling Marky and catching some Zzzz's.

We had to be careful and protective of Marky because his immunity level was still low. We didn't have a lot of people around him or handling him for the first month or so. I was home on maternity leave for three months and was planning to return to work in early September. I reached an agreement with my supervisor to work in the office a few days a week and work from home a couple of days. Mark's Aunt Kathleen volunteered to watch Marky on the days that I went into the office. I was very grateful for her offer because putting him in a traditional daycare situation was not an option. With his heart condition and the pending surgery to come later that fall, we needed to do our best to keep him as healthy as possible. I would drop him off at Aunt Kathleen's house in the morning and drive to Philly to the Wharton School where I worked in the Leadership Program. This was a job I really enjoyed because I had my own office, autonomy with my schedule, and could work at my own pace. My supervisor was awesome. She understood the plight of a young mother who also wanted a career and offered me a flexible schedule to help me to achieve work-life balance. She made me feel as if I could have the best of both worlds.

My husband set me up to work from home. The nursery was a large bedroom on the second floor only a few feet away from our master bedroom. A portion of the room was designated for my home office. The desktop computer sat on my corner desk flanked by a two-drawer filing cabinet and a shelf for office supplies. When necessary, I could use the fax machine in Mark's home office, which was initially set up for his IT administration business in the mid-1990s. Mark was passionate about his sole proprietorship, and his clientele was beginning to grow. However, Mark made the difficult decision to deactivate his business. In 2000, he left the Wharton School position for a promotion at Rutgers University in New Brunswick, New Jersey, to maintain a steady income and benefits. We discussed at length how we would operate as a family moving forward. With Marky's special needs, we knew we needed a solid income, good (medical) benefits, and the flexibility for me to not work if necessary.

I continued to work a hybrid schedule in this role for four months. It was becoming increasingly difficult for me to maintain. I was often functioning on broken sleep because Marky was not sleeping through the night yet. Although I enjoyed getting out of the house and engaging with the society of working professionals, I found myself in a conundrum. Should I try to balance working outside of the home with parenting my baby who had special needs? He was gaining weight at a slow rate, not even at ten pounds yet. But by the time the heart surgery came around in early December, I knew that my devotion needed to be primarily on Marky. So at the end of November, I resigned as a full-time employee. However, my supervisor did not have a replacement person yet and asked me to stay on as a consultant until we could find my replacement. So I worked up to twenty hours a week, mostly from home.

In December, we took Marky to A. I. duPont Hospital for Children in Wilmington, Delaware, for his first cardiac surgery with Doctor Norwood. This doctor was well-known for a procedure he developed called the Norwood procedure, which was a three-part series of heart surgeries. Marky was getting part one. We were extremely nervous for our six-month-old son, but the social worker, Judy, kept us informed every step of the way of what was happening in the operating room. My cousin, Nat, and his wife, Jackie, came to be with us at the hospital, and we all went out to the Olive Garden restaurant for lunch to eat and to try to keep our minds off worrying about Marky. I could barely eat my food. As much as I usually enjoy the buttery garlic bread sticks, I couldn't even taste the food. I kept looking at my watch and checking the phone to see if the hospital had called. We prayed and prayed that the surgery would be successful, and it was. Five hours later, we visited Marky in the cardiac intensive care unit (CICU) and found him stretched out on an infant bed still asleep, with all kinds of wires connected to him. Thank the

Lord he made a full recovery and we were able to take him home after two weeks, just in time for Christmas.

Instead of our typical Christmas gatherings with both sides of the family, this year needed to be different. Since Marky was recovering from open heart surgery, once again, his protection was our number one priority. I stayed home with the baby. Mark went to his family's dinner, and they enjoyed the traditional Christmas song fest with his mom and brothers. The annual Washington Christmas song fest was filled with lots of cheer, exaggerated melodies, modified words, and oftentimes wrong notes. It was hilarious, to say the least. They recorded it so I could watch it later, and, boy, did I laugh hard. Mom Rita and my brother-in-law, Michael, returned to our house with Mark bearing Christmas gifts and food from the family dinner. Although it was quiet, it was still a Merry Christmas. After all, my husband and I were together with our baby son, who had overcome two surgeries that year. We had much to be thankful for.

In the new year, I was trying to settle into being a stay-at-home mom. However, I was feeling disconnected from the larger society and was not satisfied. Mark came home from work in the evenings after an hour-plus commute drive and would put his feet up and ask me, "What's for dinner?" and "What did you do all day?" I was bothered by his questioning, and I nagged him about helping with the housework and helping out with Marky. I didn't consider that he was exhausted from commuting to New Brunswick every day and working full-time. This certainly caused some friction in our marriage.

Allow me to be transparent with you. I was apprehensive about becoming a stay-at-home mom because I was so used to engaging in the workforce and advancing my education and skills through professional development opportunities. I was afraid of losing my identity, and I didn't feel like I was contributing anything of value to the family. I felt a sense of pride when I could introduce myself with a fancy job title and the list of degrees I had earned. I wasn't satisfied with just saying I'm a mom. This was an internal struggle I dealt with for months. I found some help along the way when I made some key connections with other stay-at-home moms like myself for support and companionship.

In the year 2000, approximately ten babies were born in our congregation at Abundant Life Fellowship Church. Let's just say that our church fully exemplified being fruitful and multiplying. Our new church building and fully equipped nursery came at the perfect time because the nursery had full enrollment that year. We started an informal "mommy and me" support group that met twice a month in each other's homes. Some of the mothers decided to be stay-at-home moms long-term, and others decided they wanted to return to the workforce after maternity leave ended. This was a fun outlet and a great way to stay connected with other moms and not feel isolated by ourselves at home. I could have easily just kept myself in the house and focused only on Marky and his medical issues, but I probably would have gone stir-crazy. The older children who weren't in school yet also enjoyed having a playdate with other kids their age. Our sessions comprised a light lunch and a discussion topic. The time spent together was a rewarding source of socialization, information, and encouragement to help us advance as young mothers.

I also joined a group called Mocha Moms, Inc., a national support group for mothers of color through all phases of motherhood. There were local chapters for in-person interaction and online support as well. The Burlington County Chapter enjoyed weekly reading hours at the Barnes & Noble bookstore in Moorestown with Miss Alice. On one Friday a month, there was a "girls' night out" just for the moms to meet for social interaction and encouragement. We did fun things like take a boat ride and have elaborate potlucks in our homes. I remember when we had an OB-GYN doctor join us for a session on women's health care. Some of our Mocha Moms were entrepreneurs and would lead teaching sessions on starting a home-based business. We learned how to make money and save money while being stay-at-home moms. Other times were to simply let our hair down, laugh, listen, cry, and comfort each other. These were all activities I looked forward to and treasured. It occurred to me that I could be a valuable contributor to my household while enjoying being a stay-at-home mom.

In the fall of 2001, I became an executive assistant to a friend who had a communications business. Marky was stable enough that I could work part-time outside of the home. He was not on any medication at this time, and he did not need any heart monitoring. During this time, my sister-in-law Lila was operating a daycare business in her home. I began taking Marky there on a part-time basis. He enjoyed spending time with his Aunt Lila and his cousins, Amber and Aleya. They got to know each other better and got along with one another. Taking turns wearing Uncle Fields' sharp dress hats, crawling on the floor, and watching cartoons on TV were some of their favorite pastimes.

Turning a Corner

Those songs of victory, prayers, and Scripture affirmations sure carried me through that first year of Marky's medical challenges. Thanks be unto God, Marky came through them all. I was grateful to report his spleen worked fine, his digestive system was fully repaired, his heart was regulated, and he would not require any more heart surgery for now. It is also worth mentioning that I took Marky to see a neurologist while he was an infant because his feet, legs, hands, and fingers were very stiff and turned inward when he was born. The only explanation the neurologist gave was that Marky somehow showed mild symptoms of cerebral palsy but they had not fully manifested. I was shocked to hear this. At the recommendation of the doctor, the physical therapist designed custom made braces for his ankles, legs, and hands, which he wore a certain number of hours per day. Marky was finally discharged from physical therapy after several months.

At one-year-old, he was now up to speed on his gross motor skills such as clapping his hands, standing up, crawling, sitting down, and rolling over on his own. Could it be that our prayers intervened while he was still developing in the womb and stopped the full manifestation of cerebral palsy in Marky? I don't have any other explanation for this. I count this as another miracle from God. And *finally*, Marky was sleeping through the night. I thanked God for His healing power and entrusting Marky to us. It was truly a privilege and a pleasure to be his guardian.

When Marky turned two, he joined his cousin Alexis at God's Little Angels Preschool. He arrived at preschool knowing how to talk and how to recognize the alphabet. Marky developed a close friendship with Ariana, a cute little girl who also attended our church. She and Marky enjoyed playing together for hours. As they became best friends, we became friends with her parents. Bobby and Deirdre Cobb have been very close friends ever since our kids were toddlers.

By the middle of August, Marky had become a big brother to his baby sister, Naomi, whom we affectionately called Mimi. I was fortunate to have a normal pregnancy this go round. Just to be sure our little girl was developing normally, I went to duPont at Jefferson again for a fetal echocardiogram a few months before she was born. Thank goodness, her heart looked perfect; no signs of abnormalities. However, her ultrasound revealed that she would be a thumb sucker. Hopefully that would be the most difficult physical challenge we would encounter with Mimi.

Marky liked having a little sister and was anxious for her to grow up enough so they could play together. When Naomi was born, it gave me even more of a reason to continue being a work-from-home mom. I continued to juggle parenting with working part-time from home. I felt like I was a better mother to my kids when I could compartmentalize and designate certain times when I was working. A little over a year later, with Marky's health intact and Naomi ready for daycare, I updated my resume, landed a job, and started working full time at the University of Pennsylvania in December 2003.

My new role at the Wharton Executive Education program afforded me the pleasure of meeting some smart and influential people. I enhanced my skillset with additional tools and resources that padded my resume. I enjoyed sporting my business casual wardrobe. One of the perks of this job was the daily catered lunch for staff, complete with a variety of beverages. It was a small department of just five employees, so we got to know one another pretty well. Overall, it was a good job. I was working at an Ivy League institution with world-renowned faculty, producing cutting-edge knowledge and the next generation of leaders in various industries.

On the other hand, there were some downsides. The time I spent with my kids each day had dwindled down to about three hours. I had to squeeze in some quality time of playing, cuddling, and sometimes disciplining in the same timeframe with cooking, eating, cleaning up, and preparing their meals and clothes for the next day.

Where did my husband Mark fit into this complex puzzle? Mark was also working full time while pursuing his master's degree at Rutgers University. On the nights Mark wasn't in class, we spent time together after the kids were in bed and the house quieted down. He helped out around the house when he could, but he was also short on disposable time as he sought after more education and career advancement.

I looked forward to the weekends, when our schedules were less stringent, but the to-do list was still long. I called it the amazing race, like the popular TV show. We had to grocery shop, do laundry, complete housekeeping and yardwork, and run various other errands. Sunday morning worship was a time of refreshing in God's presence and connecting with our friends. We would also carve out some family time after church to visit with our parents and extended relatives.

Then it was back to the grind, back to the rat race on Monday mornings. I found myself speeding on Route 295 every day to commute to work on time and to pick up Mimi from the daycare, often arriving with only a few minutes to spare. The one good thing about those commutes was I used the time to listen to talk radio and to talk to family members I hadn't connected with in a while. I was exhausted though. Lunchtime naps in a nearby common study area for graduate students became the norm. I felt guilty every time I asked for some time off from work to do something with my kids. Then I would feel guilty when I wasn't there for my kids, even though we had a supportive village who would step up and help out when they could.

We rode this merry-go-round ride for almost a year, and finally my husband said, "Honey, I want you to come home. The kids and I need you to come home. We need a better quality of life." After we calculated the expenses associated with me working full-time outside of the home, the small amount of money I netted didn't make up for the lack of quality of life that had become our norm.

I resigned from my job at the Wharton School and came home to acquire the most meaningful title I've ever held, the CHO—Chief Home Officer. (Thank you to my Mocha Moms inspiration.) This was another answer to my prayers. I had a new perspective of being a stay-at-home mom. Before, I thought it was a chore and that my career was stifled by this added responsibility. I now found it to be a privilege that I could focus on my marriage, my family, my home, and tend to my personal needs as a woman. I could do the things that really mattered the most to me. I had aspirations of starting my own real estate investing company, sharing more intimate times with my husband, singing more at church, and of course, spending quality time with the kids.

My kids were doing better with my focus on them. Although Marky ended up getting silver crowns on all eight molars due to the bad dental hygiene (while I was busy working), he got better. I started trying to stay on top of that. The next school year, Marky adjusted well to kindergarten at his new school, Bernice Young Elementary School. He was student of the month in September 2005. Naomi was ninety percent potty trained, and we managed to get her to stop sucking her thumb. That was a tremendous feat. It warmed my heart to see her enjoying gymnastic classes. Yes, our household income decreased, but the rewards of less stress and more quality time with my husband and kids far outweighed the money. I finally embraced my role as the CHO and used it to make a positive deposit that is still paying out dividends today.

I understand many moms are supporting their children by themselves, or they may be the breadwinner in the household and cannot afford or don't have the option not to work. In today's society, there are many work-from-home options to make a decent living and fulfill your number one job of being a parent.

For instance, my sister Monica took matters into her own hands (literally) as a single mom raising both her daughter and goddaughter. She is a licensed and skilled cosmetologist who styles women, men, girls, and boys' hair by creating beautiful hairstyles that build their confidence. She also loves working with children and has anointed hands to make the most delicious banana pudding, jewelry, balloon arches, party decorations, home décor, and the list goes on and on. Initially, she was working in other hair salons and found herself struggling to balance raising her two girls while working evenings and weekends. She had family around to pitch in as needed, but primarily, she had to do the heavy lifting. My sister decided to take in hair clients at home, where she could also provide care for her growing daughters. Monica took her experience of working in a daycare and launched her own in-home daycare. She is running both home-based businesses, raised her daughter and goddaughter, and earned a degree at the same time. She thought outside of the box and leveraged her many talents and skills to build multiple streams of income while working from home.

There is no fixed answer to this question of working or not working. All women need to survey their resources, their family's needs, and their own ambitions to see what will work best for them. The article "Should Moms Work or Stay at Home?"[3] mentions various studies that provide science to support all moms, both working and at home. This article underlined some of the very feelings I had as I explored and tried to find the right fit for me. Overwhelmingly, more moms with kids living at home (about seventy-one percent) hold another job other than mommy. On the other hand, the number of moms staying home with their kids had risen since the 1999 study, when only twenty-three percent of moms did so. Just find out what works best for you.

Challenge:

1. Read the article "Should Moms Work or Stay at Home?"
2. What is driving you to want to work? What is driving you to want to stay at home with your kids?

3. Discuss this with your significant other and decide what will be best for your family. God will honor your desire to do what is best. He will provide everything you need.

4. While you're in your season of mothering young kids, find a mothers' support group such as Moms of Preschoolers (MOPS), Mocha Moms, Inc., and other parenting support groups on Facebook.

PRAYER FOCUS: Lord God, I thank You for the gift of my children, for they are a heritage from You (Psalm 127:3). Please guide my thoughts and help me to decide how to spend my time in this season of my life.

CHAPTER 4

YOLO—You Only Live Once

This is the day the Lord has made; we will rejoice and be glad in it.
—Psalm 118:24 (NKJV)

Marky had an easy-going spirit, big brown eyes with long lashes, and a warm smile that would light up any room. He was a special kid who attracted admirers young and old. We never had trouble getting a sitter for him, because Marky was such a good kid and a joy to be around. His bubbly laughs were infectious, and spread cheer to anyone in his presence. He was everybody's sweetheart. He was enamored by the drummers in our church band and watched them closely. Marky tried to imitate them at home on his drum set provided by his godfather, while listening to Kirk Franklin's song *Hosanna (Forever)*. Marky had developed several other hobbies, one of which was playing soccer.

In the summer of 2005, Marky was five years old and Mimi was almost three years old. I found a little tots' soccer club at one of the local parks in the area to give week-long soccer camps. I registered Marky for the camp and brought Mimi along with us. Only a few kids came out for the camp, so Marky received lots of small group and individual instruction on the basic skills of playing soccer. I sat under the nearby tree on a blanket to catch some relief from the hot sun rays, snapping some photos while the kids had the three-hour session. Mimi had so much energy that she was often out on the field with the other kids too. The coach didn't seem to mind at all and included her in the activities. They both enjoyed learning the sport. Mimi's hair was styled in a high bun full of her natural curls with beads of sweat on her face. It seemed to be the coolest hairstyle for her during those steamy days. On the last day of the camp, the athletes received a soccer t-shirt and a brand-new soccer ball. Then they had the opportunity to show off the skills they learned that week, such as kicking the ball while running. Not only did Marky get to exhibit his new soccer skills, but Mimi was invited out to the field to show off what she had learned as well. I couldn't believe it because I did not pay a registration fee for her. However, she was included in the camp, and that began Mimi's love of soccer.

At the end of August, I saw that the Willingboro Recreation Department offered a Little League soccer program for the fall season. Since Marky had a good introduction to soccer and he expressed an interest in playing, I decided to call to inquire about it. However, it was a little too late and all the teams were full. I was told if I found a team with an open spot, I could try to get my son on that team.

So out to the soccer field we went that night. I was pleasantly surprised that one of the coaches attended my church, and we were also in the same Mocha Moms Chapter. I asked her if she had any open slots available. The teams were co-ed at this age level, so there was a mix of boys and girls out on the field. Marky knew the coach's son because of a few Mocha Moms family events we had attended together. Technically, no player slots were available; however, I noticed that she could use some administrative help with the soccer team. I offered to be an assistant coach who would be responsible for maintaining the team roster, the contact information for all the players' parents and coaches. I would send weekly emails to confirm practice and game dates, times, and locations. She was then convinced to let my son play as long as I was volunteering my time as well. This is an example of how your gifts will make room for you.

As a child, I never played soccer. To be honest, the soccer program didn't heavily recruit the black kids in my town. So I did not know any of the rules except to try to kick the ball into the goal. I went home and told my husband that Marky was now on the soccer team. He couldn't believe it and was wondering what prompted me to sign him up. I really didn't have a profound reason why, but I just felt the urgency to give Marky this opportunity to play on a team. I was a stay-at-home mom at the time, taking care of Marky and Mimi. I wanted them to be active and engaged. I made sure he had a good pair of sneakers and shin guards to wear. The soccer ball he received from the soccer camp came in handy.

The Orange Crush team had fun that season, and I learned quite a bit about soccer. My duties as an assistant coach extended beyond the administrator role. I found myself out on the field doing drills and kicking the balls with the players. But what I loved the most was talking to the other parents, coordinating who would bring the orange slices and juice boxes to the next game.

Marky had fun learning how to be on a team. One cold Saturday morning at Mill Creek Park, Orange Crush was playing another team. It was probably mid-November, and the grass was frosted over from the colder temperatures. The kids' t-shirts were big enough that we put the T-shirt over top of their winter jackets to help them stay warm while meeting the uniform requirement. The family came out to support little Marky. My parents were sitting on the sidelines with their lawn chairs cheering him on and drinking their hot cocoa. Marky's godparents, Donald and Katya, happened to be at the park exercising when they saw Mark Sr. at the field and realized that Marky was one of the players. So they were also along the sidelines now cheering for the Orange Crush team.

I can remember the time when Marky was running the opposite way from the ball. He was actually running the wrong way. And we kept yelling, "Go back the other way, Marky!" Nonetheless, he couldn't help but smile and giggle as he was running in the direction he wanted to go. So we laughed as well. Each of us was just tickled that he could be out there running and playing such a normal activity with the other children even though he had such an abnormal start to life. We all got a kick out of that moment.

At the end of the season, there was a banquet to honor the players and the coaches at the JFK Recreation Center. Marky was so proud of himself. He smiled and looked at his tall golden trophy with pride. I was surprised to also receive a plaque thanking me for my dedication as the assistant coach for the team. We took photos to capture the memories of the teams' accomplishments. It felt good.

By the way, there are good reasons why kids should receive participation awards for sports. Some folks believe only the champions should win trophies. However, I disagree. Every child needs to know what it feels like to be recognized for their efforts and contributions to the team. They need to feel a sense of belonging and success. When they experience this at a young age, as they get older and face tougher competition, they will work harder so they can achieve it again—not just in sports, but in various activities such as school and work. When they have tasted success, they will strive to do what it takes to get the reward.

Shortly after the awards night, Marky had another cardiology appointment. The doctor was very concerned about a leaky mitral valve of the heart. Marky had not needed cardiac surgery since he was six months old, but we were nearing the time for him to have the surgery to repair the leaky valve. It turns out that the cardiac surgeon was unable to repair it, so they went to plan B and replaced the valve with a mechanical heart valve. Marky now had a prosthetic heart valve, which meant he would need to be on blood thinners for the rest of his life. While on a blood thinner, he couldn't play contact sports anymore.

Now it dawned on me. I realized that sometimes you just have to take chances and do something out of the ordinary. "YOLO" is a popular acronym that means "you only live once." I try to seize the moment and live my life with no regrets. I'm not always successful at that; there are a few regrets in my past. However, I try not to dwell on them. I am so glad I followed my heart and allowed my son to play soccer that season. It would be the only time he played organized sports to win a trophy and know what it was like to be a part of a team, something bigger than himself. My sacrifice of living outside of my comfort zone and becoming an assistant soccer coach afforded my son this once-in-a-lifetime opportunity.

Challenge:

1. Can you identify something you've done in the last twelve months that took you out of your comfort zone and stretched you? Was there a place you went that was extraordinary and new for you? How did you feel while you were in the moment? How do you feel after accomplishing it?

2. Set a goal of something you want to accomplish in the next three to six months. Make plans to reach your goal. Each day or week, take the necessary steps until you reach your goal. Remember, life is short and you only live once.

Prayer Focus: Heavenly Father, I thank You for sending Your Son Jesus to die for my sins so that I can enjoy life abundantly. Help me to step outside of my comfort zone and follow Your leading so I can live to my fullest potential.

CHAPTER 5

Mommy, My Heart

Be anxious for nothing, but in everything by prayer and supplication,
with thanksgiving, let your requests be made known to God;
and the peace of God, which surpasses all understanding,
will guard your hearts and minds through Christ Jesus.
—Philippians 4:6, 7 (NKJV)

It's Sunday morning. Time to wake up and go to church. "Let's go, Marky and Mimi. Time to get washed and dressed in your church clothes," I encouraged the kids. My husband and I would tag team to get the family ready in the mornings. Mark Sr. often took charge of Marky to make sure he brushed his teeth properly and brushed his hair, especially around those edges. He made sure Marky's suit was fitting just right and helped him to straighten his clip-on tie. I had the honor of getting myself and little miss Naomi ready. We called her Mimi for short. I gave her this cute nickname right after she was born to avoid the natural inclination to call her Sha-nay-nay, a wildly popular character on the Martin Lawrence sitcom. I just didn't want her associated with this funny, but over the top, female, played by Lawrence himself. Overseeing Mimi was a full-time job. She had lots of energy and was very quick-moving. I stopped wearing my fancy high-heeled shoes to church once she learned how to sprint. Two-inch pumps were my normal go-to in this season of life so I could keep up with my little girl, who was eager to be free from holding my hand. I had to make sure her hair was touched up, adding a little hair grease around the edges to prevent dryness and add some sheen. Mimi's hair was almost always done by her Aunt Monica, my younger sister, a gifted hairstylist. Naomi's hair was in a fancy cornrowed style. She enjoyed flinging around her colorful beads at the ends of her long braids. I liked it because it was easy to keep up by putting a stocking cap on it at night and brushing up the edges in the morning. It kept us moving on our often-busy mornings.

We attended Abundant Life Fellowship Church (ALFC) in Edgewater Park, NJ just about every Sunday for about ten years. We joined when the church was celebrating its first anniversary. The ALFC congregation was meeting at the Willingboro High School auditorium at the time. We had several family members there and gained a host of friends. My mother-in-law, Rita, and Mark's oldest brother, Michael, attended the church. Mom Rita raved about the rich worship experiences and life-changing word she was hearing week after week. We finally decided to visit, and much to our delight, we enjoyed it too and eventually decided to join the fellowship. A few years later, my brother-in-law, Minister Darryl, his lovely wife, Lila, and their daughters joined the fellowship as well.

We attended the 10:30 a.m. service at church and had a joyous time in the presence of the Lord. Our kids attended Koinonia Kids Ministry in the educational wing of the church. They enjoyed the Bible classes with kids their own age. Their teachers were friendly and made the Bible stories come alive with lessons easy to understand. Plus, the kids looked forward to the snacks they received each time they attended. In the main sanctuary, Rev. Dr. Eve Fenton preached the message called "The Beloved Father." It was the familiar account of the Prodigal Son. After the service, we greeted our family members and many of our church friends who had really become family to us during our decade-long membership.

Our kids looked forward to seeing their many friends at the church as well. Just a few weeks prior, Marky spent the night at the Cook family home for his best friend Miles' birthday sleepover. I was a little nervous about him staying overnight, especially with his daily regimen of medications. However, Terry and Kecia wanted to make their son's wish come true by having his closest friends over and insisted that Marky stay overnight too. Thank goodness Marky did not have any problems at all. They made some lasting memories that evening.

Photo Shoot

We returned home after church and changed our clothes before having a light lunch. The kids played in the house for a little bit. Then they took a short nap on the sofas in the living room while I straightened up the house and slow-roasted some barbecue ribs for dinner. After a few hours, it was time to get dressed again. This time we were dressing up to take our annual family Christmas photo. I made sure our outfits were color-coordinated. Mimi wore a maroon-colored dress embellished with a rhinestone belt buckle. Marky was sharp in a maroon button-down shirt and a tan pin-striped vest with a maroon and tan tie. Mark wore a brown sports jacket and white shirt with maroon accents in the tie. I wore a blush pink two-piece dress with gold accents running throughout the pattern. I added a blush color bow to Mimi's hair adorned with multi-color beads. We were all set for our photo shoot at the nearby Sears portrait studio at the Burlington Center Mall on Route 541.

After our photo session ended, we were in the hallway preparing to leave when some familiar faces appeared at the side entrance.

It was the Goodman family, who also attended Abundant Life Fellowship Church. We exchanged greetings and complimented each other on the nice outfits. This family was also known for giving out Christmas photo cards each year. They were dressed from head to toe to take their photos as well. We gave our hugs, wished them well, and left the store.

We headed home and immediately changed into our pajamas. I was warming up the sides that would go along with the barbecue ribs. Everyone was hungry and ready to eat. When we sat down together at our kitchen table, we had a tradition we practiced with the kids. Right after we said the blessing over the meal, we took turns around the table to say what we were thankful for. I remember Marky said he was thankful he got to spend Thanksgiving with the family. I thanked God we didn't spend the holiday in the hospital. As we ate our delicious dinner, we thought about how much fun we had at Thanksgiving dinner at my brother George's home in a neighboring town just three days prior. We enjoyed having large family dinners whenever we could, because we had such a good time. But we were tired of the turkey leftovers, so that's why I opted to cook pork ribs falling off the bones, drenched in sweet and savory barbecue sauce. They were finger-licking good to the last bite. We cleared the dishes off the table, and I washed up the dinner dishes.

Playtime

The kids went off to play in the house. I felt a vibration on my right hip. It was my cell phone buzzing as a reminder that it was 8 p.m., time for Marky to take some medicine. I opened the kitchen cabinet door nearest the sink to look at the full list of daily medications for Marky. Nine medications were listed that helped to keep this young, energetic boy's heart going. I called for Marky to come into the kitchen to take the Coumadin. He knew what to expect. I used the pill cutter to split the pills in half so it would be easier for him to swallow. At six-years-old, he had become a pro at swallowing pills. He did it better than some adults I know, including myself. Marky took his meds and went back to playing.

Mark Sr. had just retreated to the basement, otherwise known as Eagles Country, to watch the Philadelphia Eagles play the Indianapolis Colts. He wanted to be settled in his green plush recliner chair by 8:15 p.m. for kickoff. Mark was hoping they would reverse the losing streak they were on and beat the Colts.

On the main floor of the house, Naomi was chasing Marky around the house—through the dining room, into the living room, and around the foyer, which led to the kitchen and back into the dining room. Marky was giggling so much and trying his best not to get tagged by Naomi. She was known to be the entertainer in the family and was ready to have fun at a moment's notice. They enjoyed playing with each other.

A Turn for the Worst

Suddenly, as Marky rounded the corner from the foyer into the kitchen, I heard him yell, "Mommy, my heart!" His hand was on his chest, and he broke rank and ran through the kitchen and into the family room.

I ran after him, grabbed him close to me, and put my hand on his chest. His heart was beating so fast I couldn't count the number of beats.

He yelled, "Mommy, my heart, my heart hurts!"

Immediately, he passed out in my arms and I carefully laid him on the floor. Thank goodness I was there to catch him; otherwise, he could have hit his head on the tile floor in front of the fireplace. I yelled to Naomi, "Go get your dad. Go get your dad out of the basement."

Naomi didn't know exactly what was going on, but she knew playtime was over. She backed up near the loveseat and was frozen. I could tell that she was scared. She could hear my frantic pleas for help. I grabbed the cordless telephone and quickly dialed 911 for help. I told them my six-year-old son had just collapsed with a fast-beating heart, and we needed help right away.

Naomi came back to the family room but without her dad. She was flustered and said, "He won't come. He won't listen to me, mom."

And while I was on the phone with 911, I left Marky's side and ran to the basement stairs and yelled at the top of my lungs, "Mark, get up here now! Marky collapsed. I'm on the phone with 911."

Mark was in disbelief and ran up the stairs quickly. I was already back on my knees next to Marky. The 911 operator asked me if anyone there knew CPR. And I thought for a second and said, "Yeah, yeah, I do! I know CPR, but it's been a little while. You're gonna have to talk me through it." So I listened intently to the instructions the operator gave me. The CPR training I previously had was starting to come back to my mind.

I attended training back in the late spring because I was the health coordinator for Abundant Life's church summer camp. This was my second year to be certified to perform CPR and first aid. However, I never anticipated that I'd have to give CPR to my own child. My mind was racing frantically, and I was so nervous and afraid that I would lose my son that night. I put the phone on speaker and sat it down right next to Marky's head. I felt the adrenaline kick in, and I began giving Marky chest compressions and mouth-to-mouth resuscitation as instructed by the dispatcher. I was trained to use a protective barrier, but a few minutes had already passed, and I knew from my training that every second counted. Without oxygen to the brain for ten minutes or so, there could be permanent damage. Plus, this was my son. He came from my body, so I was not afraid that he had a runny nose. I would do whatever it took to save my son's life. I continued giving CPR for a couple of minutes.

Mark answered the front door when the police and paramedics arrived and let them inside. I explained what happened, and they took over doing CPR trying to revive Marky. I saw his body jerk as he made a big gasp. He wore the green military fatigue button-down pajama shirt with matching pants given to him by my aunt and uncle some months ago during the previous hospital stay. He was wearing one of my favorite pajamas, but it didn't really matter at this time. The paramedics took scissors and cut the shirt wide open so they could expose his chest and begin compressions. The AED machine was used twice to try to revive his heart.

I called my brother-in-law Darryl, told him what happened, and asked him to come quickly. I was crying and very upset by then. I hung up the phone at the police officer's request so they could collect information from me. The paramedics asked me what kind of medicine Marky was taking, and I began to rattle off the list of prescriptions from off the top of my head. I later took the list that was taped inside the kitchen cabinet and gave it to them so they would have an accurate record of Marky's medications and doses.

My sister, Monica, must have sped all the way to the house because she was there just a few minutes after I called her. She told me later that when she rounded the corner at Route 541 and Kelly Drive, she thought her silver Ford Taurus was going to flip over. Thank goodness she and her daughter, Alexis, arrived safely. I didn't even think twice about changing out of my tiger-striped pajamas pant set. Every second mattered, and I didn't have time to change clothes. I asked Monica to go upstairs to grab my socks and shoes so I could go to the hospital. She also helped Naomi get her shoes and jacket on.

Mark secured the latch on the storm door to keep it open. As the paramedics carried Marky out to the porch on the gurney, Darryl arrived and was crossing the front lawn toward the porch. He was praying as he walked up. He'd also been watching the Eagles game when I called, but he didn't hesitate. He told his wife, Lila, what happened, grabbed his coat and keys, and drove as fast as he could to our house. He probably broke all kinds of traffic laws to get there quickly; he doesn't even remember the drive. He only remembers praying the whole way there. But thank God he made it to our house safely. When Darryl arrived, he was in a state of shock as he saw his nephew looking lifeless on the gurney. Darryl could tell by the facial expressions of the paramedics that things were not looking good for Marky.

As the gurney was being carried over the three concrete front steps, the paramedic shouted, "Hold on, Hold on!" They suddenly stopped moving, and it was silent. Darryl was dreading that pause. He continued to quietly pray. "I think I've got a heartbeat! It's faint, but I've got a heartbeat," said the paramedic. We had a brief sigh of relief. We knew Marky wasn't out of the woods yet, but we knew he was still alive. Then the paramedics moved him quickly toward the ambulance, which was parked in the bottom half of the driveway behind our two parked vehicles. They carefully put Marky in the ambulance. And I begged Mark to ride in the ambulance with him. "Don't leave him by himself." I cried. Mark had his jacket in his hand and climbed in the back of the ambulance to be with our son. I jumped in the car with Darryl, and he drove me to Rancocas Valley Hospital. It was less than ten minutes away from our house. We didn't follow the ambulance but went a different route, only to meet the ambulance at an intersection around the corner. Darryl yielded to the ambulance, and we followed behind. I was busy calling my parents, my brother, and my pastors and cell group members to let them know and ask for their sincere prayers of healing.

At the hospital, the paramedics took him right into the emergency room. The doctors and medical team were waiting for his arrival. I was sent to the triage nurse to give our contact and insurance information. The doctor needed more information about Marky's health. I remembered I kept a small sticky note in my wallet, which listed about nine abnormalities Marky persisted with. I even had his cardiologist sketch a small diagram of the anatomy of Marky's heart on the note. The edges of the note were visibly worn from being folded and carried in my wallet for almost six years. Although this cardiac arrest came out of nowhere, I was ready for it. God had prepared me for it in ways I didn't realize until later. I gave the 5"x3" yellow sticky note to the doctors, and someone photocopied it right away. They were extremely grateful to have this information. I called the CICU at duPont Hospital, and surprisingly, no one answered the phone. I couldn't believe it. Then I called the front desk. However, since it was after visiting hours, they had a voicemail system set up. I left a message. A few minutes later, Dr. Anisman called me. His voice was calm and reassuring. "Mrs. Washington, I received your voicemail message, and I am sorry to hear that Mark went into cardiac arrest. I'm also sorry no one answered the phone in the CICU. That should have never happened." I explained to Marky's cardiologist what happened. And then I walked over to the room where the medical team was working on Marky. I could see through the window a huge syringe sticking up out of his left shin. Oh my God, that looked like it hurt. I handed my cell phone to the lead ER doctor so he could talk to Dr. Anisman. They discussed Marky's condition and came up with an action plan to get him stable. The ER doctors were thinking the next plan of action was to get Marky sent to Children's Hospital of Philadelphia (CHOP). However, I was adamant that Marky was to be transferred to A.I. duPont Hospital in Wilmington, Delaware. Although it was further away, that was his hospital. They knew him there, and I had confidence they would take care of him best.

As we waited in the lobby area, members of our church started showing up one by one. They were deeply concerned and were praying for us. I recalled several church members of our Apostolic (pastoral) Council and our close friends from the couples' cell group were there surrounding us with comfort and support. Monica was also at the hospital. She was keeping Mimi and Alexis occupied while we waited for an update from the doctor.

I felt covered. I felt lifted up. My mind and body felt partially numb, but I had a sense of clarity. I knew what we needed to do to advocate for our son's care. Although the triage nurse didn't want to bother to ask me for my insurance card, I insisted that she take my card to make a copy for the records. I needed them to order every medication and treatment possible to save my child's life, and I didn't want insurance to be the hold-up. The emergency room's medical team used their expertise and worked swiftly to stabilize Marky. I knew we were in for a long night.

CHALLENGE:

1. What is your first instinct when life takes a sudden twist?

2. How do you handle quick transitions in life?

3. Think about how you respond in moments of crises. Are you frantic, emotional, calm, methodical? How does your response affect the mood of the environment?

Prayer Focus: Loving Father, help me to exhibit Your character even in the worst situations I face. Holy Spirit, I need You to guide my footsteps and my thoughts. Thank You for being Jehovah Shammah, the God who is always with me.

CHAPTER 6

Faith Tested

Now faith is confidence in what we hope for and assurance about what we do not see.
—Hebrews 11:1 (NIV)

The hospital staff ordered a helicopter to pick up Marky and transferred him to the children's hospital that night. I called my cousin Nat Milton, who lived in Delaware, and told him what happened. I asked Nat to meet Marky at the hospital. We would soon follow but needed to go home, pack a bag, and close down our house.

Nat, his wife Jackie, and Uncle Nate Milton Sr. were at the hospital when the helicopter arrived. I gave instructions for the hospital staff to give them permission to be with Marky as he was being transported to the cardiac unit. I wanted family there with him in case anything else were to happen. Nat was an ordained minister of the gospel, and I knew he was a man of prayer and the right person to be there with Marky. Nat told me they rode on the elevator with Marky. He prayed over Marky during the transport to the cardiac center. My heart was comforted knowing that family was with him; he was not alone.

We packed a bag for Mimi and put it in an empty can on our backyard deck so that Monica could pick it up the next day. She took Mimi home with her overnight. Mark and I each packed a big suitcase. I knew this would be a long stay, so I packed enough for a week. We grabbed our laptops, phone book, journal, and other items I knew I would need to access while in the hospital. We turned down the heat on the thermostat, loaded the car, and locked the house. Mark drove us to the hospital, which took about an hour and fifteen minutes. When we arrived, it was after 2 a.m. The nurse on duty met us in the corridor as she saw us walking through the entrance of cardiac unit 2B and showed us to our room. The doctors met with us shortly after we arrived and told us they were watching Marky closely. The next twenty-four hours were critical. We had to wait and see how he would progress.

My husband's laptop was sitting on the edge of the bed open. There were two twin beds in the large room that we pushed together to make one king-sized bed for Mark and me to stay overnight. I pulled the chair up to the side of the bed as a makeshift desk. It served as my temporary headquarters while my son's life laid in the balance down the hallway and around the corner in the CICU. I emailed our family and friends to let them know what was going on. I wore comfortable pajamas and soft, warm slippers to avoid feeling the coldness of the hard, tiled floor of the hospital room we were assigned to.

Monday, November 27, 2006, 2:30 p.m.

Dear Family & Friends,

With great sadness we must inform you that our son, Marky, experienced heart failure last night and was taken to the emergency room, where he was resuscitated. Marky was then airlifted to the A. I. duPont Hospital for Children in Wilmington, DE and is currently in the intensive care unit in a coma.

The main concern the doctors have about Marky is the status of his brain function that was traumatized by the lack of oxygen during the cardiac arrest. The next 24 to 48 hours are critical for Marky to awaken and give us indications that his brain is functioning. We are asking you to join with us in prayer for Marky to awaken with his FULL mental capacity very soon.

May God bless you all and we will email you again soon with the expected praise report.

Mark & Dynita

As much as I did not like being in the hospital with a sick child, I didn't mind it as much because we were at duPont Hospital for Children. This was like the country clubs of hospitals. We were provided three meals a day from the cafeteria, where the food was actually tasty. They even had a laundry room down the hallway for the families to use, with laundry detergent and dryer sheets provided. The large patient rooms were set up for two adults to stay in the patient room while the patient received care. There was a private full bathroom and ample closet space. A tube television and VCR hung from the ceiling with enough channels to keep us updated with what was going on in the outside world and also help us escape from the nightmare we were now living.

It was the Monday after the Thanksgiving holiday, what we now know as Cyber Monday, but in 2006, most people just thought of it as the first day back to school and work after an extended weekend of family time, turkey sandwiches, sweet potato pie, and shopping sprees at the local malls. This time typically marked the four-week countdown until Christmas. Oh, how I wished this was a normal end of a four-day weekend, but instead, I found myself involuntarily enlisted into my worst nightmare. My son Marky, who was only six years old, was fighting for his life with an irregular heartbeat and declining heart function.

This place was familiar territory; it was like déjà vu. As a matter of fact, we had stayed in this very room in January of this year when Marky had his second heart surgery, the replacement of the mitral valve. So although it was sterile and cold, with bright lights and constant beeping sounds of medical machines nearby, it was homey in a weird sort of way. I purchased oversized pajamas eleven months earlier so I would feel comfortable with the medical team coming in and out of the room when caring for Marky. What was supposed to be a short, two-week hospital stay in January turned out to be a full two-and-a-half-month recovery period.

Our list of supporters and prayer warriors was growing, so in order to keep them informed, I started blogging on the CaringBridge website. It was a popular site to stay connected with family and friends during any health journey. Mark and I took turns writing posts approximately every other day. These posts gave updates on Marky's progress, listed specific prayer requests, and somehow I mustered up the strength to encourage others in their walk with the Lord. We gave thanks to God for every victory along the way and kept the faith when setbacks occurred.

It was a wild rollercoaster ride at times. Marky had another cardiac arrest when he arrived in the procedure room to get a CT (x-ray) scan. Thankfully, he was resuscitated and the CT scan showed no hemorrhaging or swelling on the brain. We watched Marky on the ventilator for weeks. He gradually began to regain consciousness and his ability to track with his eyes. I was grateful he recognized us and would try to hold our hands even though they were covered with splints holding multiple IVs in place. He was so sad because he couldn't talk, eat, or get out of bed. We kept encouraging him and telling him that he was getting better each day. I sang some of his favorite songs to him, read our affirmations with Scriptures about healing, and read him the comforting comments from our followers on the blog.

Wednesday, November 29, 2006 01:34 p.m.

Dear Marky,

You are so precious and loved soooo much by God, Jesus, Aunt Ruth, Uncle Sherrell, and cousin Kenny!!! We pray for your complete recovery and no more discomfort. Oxoxoxoxox....

Aunt Ruth
Sun City West, AZ

We were blessed to have many visitors during this time period, so we didn't feel alone. My mother, sister, and niece made regular weekend visits and would stay at the nearby Ronald McDonald House (RMH) in Wilmington, Delaware. This was a beautiful facility designed to temporarily house outpatients and their families and families of in-patients while receiving treatment at the hospital. Local organizations would provide meals on a daily basis to support the families. Lots of other donations poured into the RMH, which helped to subsidize the cost of staying there. This was such a blessing, because it was much less than the cost of staying at a hotel. I even remembered when our church couples' cell group paid us a special visit. They sang sacred Christmas songs and one of my favorite worship songs, "You Deserve the Glory," which warmed our hearts and encouraged us. The lyrics say:

"You deserve the glory and the honor.
Lord we lift our hands in worship as we lift your holy name.
You are great. You do miracles so great.
There is no one else like you."

Our faith in God was definitely tested. We relied on our friends, family members, and the prayers of people we had never met but had joined the chorus of prayers for healing Marky and strengthening his family. I could feel the prayers undergirding us and giving us the strength to stay positive, keep the faith, and smile even when we felt like crying. We did shed some tears along the way, and that's okay. I just thank God for a continuous outpouring of support, giving us hope for a better future for our son.

There were no private patient rooms in the CICU. As I walked through the automatic double doors into the large room, I could see patient beds lined along the left side. The bright primary colors throughout gave the rectangular room some much-needed cheer. Under those bright lights were fragile and immunocompromised children fighting for their lives. On the right side was the nurses' station and some small rooms that only staff entered. The medical staff could see every patient in the room from the nurses' station. They kept a close eye on every patient. Since Marky had been in the CICU for the longest and he had the most visitors, they relocated Marky to the far left of the room near the wall. He had a little more privacy because there was only one patient to the right of him. We rolled in a TV on a cart and placed it at the foot of Marky's bed. Marky's friend Katelyn and her parents brought a small Christmas tree adorned with ornaments to decorate his room and bring him some cheer. We had very few options of where to put the tree in such a small space, so we taped it down on top of the television. It could be easily moved out of the way when he was getting his various treatments and therapies throughout the day.

Day by day, week by week, we witnessed the hand of God on Marky's life. After he was gradually weaned from the ventilator to the BiPap machine and eventually to an oxygen mask, he started to smile again. We could see the contentment on his face as he watched his favorite movies and saw his dad playing the Xbox video games, which was their favorite pastime. He would try to reach for the game controller even with his arms in splints from the IVs.

He was slowly becoming responsive with body gestures and eventually started speaking with one word— Yes. Dad. Ouch. Early on Christmas morning, Marky woke up to some presents around his bed. He yelled out, "I want my dad." We were ecstatic when the nurse rushed into our room to tell us Marky was awake and talking. We quickly got dressed and went to see our Christmas miracle.

Christmas at duPont

On Christmas day, we were surrounded by our loving and faithful family members. My parents, Monica, George, Veronica, and Alexis came to Delaware to not only visit Marky but to prepare a dinner for us at the Ronald McDonald House. The staff at the RMH allowed us to reserve a private conference room. The family brought in festive table cloths, ham, mac 'n cheese, string beans, and all the fixings. Mark and I went to the RMH to eat and spend time with the family while Marky was resting.

The Washington family came to the hospital posse deep, as we used to say back in the day—Mom Rita, Gregory, Erika, Psalm, Suriah, Darryl, Lila, Amber, Aleya, and Angelina. They came bearing gifts, smiles, and good cheer. Marky wore a red plaid button-down short-sleeve shirt. His hair was a little overgrown but neatly brushed. We surrounded Marky's bed and recliner chair as we sang "We Wish You a Merry Christmas and a Happy New Year." With an IV in one arm, he needed help opening his many gifts. He received Spider-Man Mega Bloks and an electronic keyboard. Although his voice was weak and a little shaky, he waved his hand as a way of saying thank you. Marky was grinning from ear to ear, excited to see his cousins, aunts, and uncles. He raised both arms and hands as if he was directing the choir as we sang "Joy to the World." I could see his lips mouthing the words underneath his purple dinosaur oxygen mask as he tried to sing along. Naomi was dressed up like a princess with her crown and glasslike Cinderella slippers. She would introduce herself as Snow White with a tan. This would catch people off guard after they thought about it for a second but went along with this spunky little girl with a big imagination. Marky looked around the room and was just taking it all in, surrounded by his family. He loved them and he knew they loved him too.

I invited the family back to our room in the step-down cardiac unit to give Marky a little break from all the excitement. Much to their surprise, we handed out gifts to them all. They couldn't believe we had time to buy gifts for them with all that we were going through. However, I did most of the shopping on our last vacation in Martha's Vineyard.

Our close friends, the Cobb family, had invited us to join them on a week-long vacation in Oak Bluffs. We had a great time hanging out at the beach and riding tandem bicycles around the island. Marky rode with his dad and Mimi rode on my bike. One afternoon we went shopping in town and came across some boutiques with the cutest accessories. I told Mark I'd like to buy some Christmas gifts. He said, "What? Christmas? It's only August, Dynita. There is plenty of time to buy Christmas gifts." I convinced him that I would not find these unique items at such a fair price back at home in New Jersey. We had extra space in our black with gold-trimmed Ford Explorer SUV to carry them. Mark reluctantly agreed. I bought an assortment of purses, wraps, and hair accessories. I had some ideas of who I was buying for, but not exactly for all. So I bought as much as I could afford without breaking the bank and would decide later when it was time to wrap the gifts.

Little did I know we would suddenly find ourselves staying in the hospital during the holidays. So as Christmas approached, I asked Mark to bring those bags of gifts to the hospital, along with tape, scissors, and wrapping paper. I prepared the gifts for the family late in the night, as Marky slept around the corner in the CICU. There was also a Holiday Pop-Up gift shop in the lobby of the hospital about two weeks before Christmas. The hospital staff were so thoughtful. This was perfect for the parents who didn't have time to leave the hospital but wanted to pick up a gift or two for children who were hospitalized and their other children who remained at home. So believe it or not, I was somehow ready for Christmas. Even with the heavy weight I was carrying at the time, it felt good to give to others. We had received so much love and support. I wanted to bring joy to them during this season.

One other memory I want to highlight was that the local symphony orchestra came to the hospital and gave a Christmas concert. I was surprised to hear the melodious sounds as I approached the cafeteria one afternoon. There was no singing, just the harmonies of the instruments blending together. They were ministering to my heart in such a way that it brought tears to my eyes. The gift of music is powerful. So many people would tell me over the years how much they were blessed by my singing. I graciously thanked them and didn't think much of it. My family sang all the time. I sang regularly in our church choir, and every year we prepared a special cantata of beautiful songs for the season and invited the community to come. But this time, I couldn't be there. This time I wasn't the one who was giving the gift of song. I was the recipient of the musical talents of others. It blessed my soul so much.

Here is a blog post I wrote on the CaringBridge site.

Thursday, January 4, 2007, 11:46 p.m.

CHOP's Response

Hi all! Marky had another great day of progress. Each day he is getting physically stronger and has become quite the chatter box in the CICU. He looks so good.

We heard from the doctor on the Heart Transplant team at CHOP (Children's Hospital of Philadelphia) today. The good news is that they are confident they can do the heart transplant even given Marky's complex anatomy. However, they are not ready to accept Marky as a candidate for the donor-recipient list. They would like to see him make more improvements neurologically. The transplant surgery is a tremendous undertaking, which requires that he go on the heart & lung bypass machine, and they want to be sure that he is strong enough to get through it. So two people from CHOP's transplant team will visit us here at DuPont next Friday. As part of the evaluation process, they must interview the patient and the parents to make sure we are up for the challenge. Marky must also have numerous blood tests done, which will begin tomorrow.

So I am encouraged that we are taking steps toward getting Marky listed for his new heart. Once they meet Marky, they will not be able to turn him away because he exhibits so much life. He is a strong fighter who is proving he is able to overcome this challenge. With our continued prayers, he will have a total recovery and live in divine health for years to come.

Please keep the following in your prayers:

- *The Heart Transplant Evaluation Process goes smoothly.*
- *Marky will be back on his feet and walking on his own.*

- *Marky's veins are viable and able to handle all the IVs and blood draws necessary to manage his care. (His little arms and feet are so scarred from all the needles.)*
- *Marky will be able to swallow sufficiently so he can eat and drink by mouth.*
- *Continued improvements of speech and other neurological functions*
- *Continued protection from dangerous heart rhythms*
- *The heart donor and their family members—We need to cover the one who will provide the heart for Marky with prayer because it will be a heart-wrenching loss for them.*

I will keep you posted on Marky's progress over the weekend. God bless you all.

Love,
Dynita

Transfer to CHOP

Marky was transferred to CHOP in the third week of January. After getting him settled into his new environment and going through the battery of medical tests, Marky was added to the transplant list about two weeks later. We had high hopes he would receive a new heart soon. In the meantime, Marky was getting intense physical and occupational therapy and attending hospital school during the week. The hospital staff got to know Marky and our family and helped us to make a smooth transition. He was on the path to getting a new heart, but it was met with some challenges.

Here is another writing from my CaringBridge blog to share Marky's continued journey at CHOP.

Blog Post— Feb 15, 2007, 5:15 p.m.

More Good News!

Marky has been on a rollercoaster ride this week, but once again, he is an Overcomer. As of yesterday, he was reactivated on the heart transplant list. And today he was taken out of isolation. Although he still has a cough, he doesn't show any more contagious flu symptoms. Thank you, Jehovah Rophe (God Our Healer)! We're still not opening up the floodgates for visitors yet because he needs to be as healthy as possible to prepare for the transplant surgery. I'm sure you all understand.

One of the challenges Marky faced this week was that his PICC line was not working properly for blood draws, so the Renal Screening could not be completed. It is postponed until further notice. Late last night the doctors decided to remove the PICC line because there was a concern that infection was setting in. As a precaution, he is taking antibiotics. He dreaded the two IVs he had to get, but they are necessary to continue his IV medication and frequent blood draws. The dental appointment turned out to be just a consultation and examination. Something as simple as sitting in a dentist's chair is actually a challenge for Marky. He has difficulty breathing while sitting in a reclined position. We'll have to think of something creative to make him comfortable for his dental cleaning later. With all your continued prayers, Marky made it through this week.

We are so blessed to have such a strong support system. My husband and I have gotten through some tough times before, but we are the first to admit that we can't do it alone. We are so grateful for the many ways that our family and friends have pitched in to help us out. Each is unique and each is equally appreciated. Things started to really get stressful for us a week or so ago. My mother-in-law could see that we needed more help, so she followed the Lord's leading and decided to take some time off from her job. Lord, bless her for the sacrifice! She is now able to stay in Philly a couple of days a week to be with Marky while I am at home spending time with Big Mark and Naomi. And she will help out with Big Mark and Naomi on the other days when she is home and I am at the hospital. This is truly a blessing for us. Although Marky & I have to get used to being apart for longer lengths of time, it is another area of growth for us to truly lean on the Lord and trust that everything is really in His hands. Praise God for sending some relief.

Continue to pray for Marky's strength, that he will be able to endure whatever obstacles he faces during the wait for his new heart. We'll keep you all posted.

Be Blessed,
Dynita

Caring for a sick child can be an extremely stressful time whether they are in the hospital or at home. It is okay to ask for help with managing life's challenges. I was away from my home for long periods of time, and Mark did not spend much time there either because he was mostly at his job or commuting to the hospital, so no one was there to care for our house. During this time of our need, people were very generous. My neighbors would step in and clear the ice and snow around our corner property throughout the winter season. My extended family members were definitely praying for us, but they also wanted to know what tangible things they could do to help us. I thought about it for a bit. Then I sheepishly asked them if they would not mind cleaning my house. Right away, they said yes and in a week's time they coordinated a clean-up crew, equipped with supplies, and cleaned my house from top to bottom. What a blessing that was to my family! They were glad to be able to help us in this way. I was grateful for their willingness to do it. I realized I needed to delegate some responsibilities so I could focus on the priorities, the health of Marky and the rest of my family.

CHALLENGE:

Here are some tips for meeting your emotional, mental, and spiritual needs while your child is in the hospital.

1. Lean on family and friends to help out in creative ways.
2. Many hospitals offer weekly group therapy for parents, especially when there is a long-term stay.
3. Spend time in the hospital chapel for a place of solace and to pray.
4. Contact the hospital chaplains for on-site spiritual support.
5. Consider the Ronald McDonald House near your hospital to meet your basic family needs, such as lodging, meals, social spaces and programs, transportation, and local resource guides.
6. If you are not near your home house of worship, find a local house of worship to attend as time allows or attend virtual services.

PRAYER FOCUS: Lord God, thank You for holding me up when things in my life are out of my control. Your word gives me faith that You will bring me through this difficult time. Thank You for helping me not be afraid of accepting help from others.

CHAPTER 7

Happy Holidays?

Rejoice in the Lord always. Again I will say, rejoice!
—Philippians 4:4 (NKJV)

We've always been a family to celebrate the holidays and special occasions with lots of food, family, and decorations. We would hang the American flag from Memorial Day through the 4th of July for backyard barbecues. We enjoyed large Thanksgiving and Christmas Day dinners at our house. It was always a jovial time with our extended family members. The long guest list would typically include my parents Paula and George Sr., my siblings Monica and George Jr., Grandmom Sylvia, Auntie Paulette and her family, Uncle Pete, Aunt Lillian and Uncle Herb, Mom Rita, Mark's brothers, and their families. Occasionally, we would be surprised when my Pop Pop Wilbur would ride his bicycle four miles to my house. Those were the good old days.

Marky and Naomi figured out what I really meant when I said, "It's time to clean up your toys and straighten up the house." They asked, "Why? Are we having company again?" I busted out laughing. They discovered the correlation between cleaning the house with people coming over to visit. "Yes, we are having company." I smiled. They replied with excitement because they loved it as much as Mark and I did.

I can remember the times we hosted Philadelphia Eagles watch parties on Sunday afternoons with our friends from our church. Although football games don't qualify as holidays, they were certainly celebrated as special events because we were serious Eagles fans. Everyone had their own Eagles jersey. Before the season began, we headed down to the Forman Mills clothing store to purchase sports jerseys. This was the more affordable way for an entire family to get outfitted in our favorite team's colors without going into debt. Marky wore #81 wide receiver, Terrell Owens, aka TO, and big Mark wore #5 quarterback, Donovan McNabb. Even Naomi dawned a pink and white jersey to be in the fan club with the #36 running back, Brian Westbrook. We were set for the season. (Fingers crossed that no one would get traded, which would mean buying a new jersey next season.)

Not only did our friends come over, but their children came over too. That meant Marky and Mimi having hours of fun with their cousins and friends their age—Amber, Aleya, Angelina, Miles, Isaiah, Tabitha, Tiffany, DJ, Domonique, Taylor, and Michael Jr. The older kids—Deja, Dionna, Jasmin, Gregory, and Terrence would look out for the younger ones. Those Sunday afternoon gatherings were like parties; kids drinking juice boxes and eating chips, pizza and hoagies. Playing video games on the "kids' TV", pulling out the toys, and in decent weather going into the backyard for some touch football were some of the highlights. Those were the days we lived for. Our corner house on Finnegans Way was often filled with good food, folks, and fun.

Now that we were practically living at the hospital with Marky, holidays were different, and not just because we weren't gathered with our extended family. Holidays were met with different expectations as we sat for days and weeks in the hospital. One of the nurses said it was common for a heart to become available for transplant around the holidays. Lifting my eyebrows in curiosity, I asked why. She said there are more vehicle accidents then.

According to a study by the University of Alabama Center for Advanced Public Safety, the holiday times are the most dangerous times to be driving on the road. Since more people are out shopping for groceries, gifts, and meeting with other family members, the increase in the number of cars on the road leads to more fatal vehicular accidents. Other factors that contribute to the increase in car accidents are that drivers are often stressed, distracted, and fatigued due to longer drives than they are used to. In addition, the number of drivers who drive under the influence of alcohol during holidays goes up as well. It makes sense that there would be more car accidents.

When we were back at duPont Hospital for Children two months prior, I met with Marky's cardiologist, Dr. Anisman, one on one in a small break room in the cardiac unit. He explained to me that Marky's heart was very unstable. It had become clear that he would need a new heart in order to extend his life. I asked the doctor about the process of getting him on the transplant list—how long it usually took and the likelihood that Marky would qualify for a heart transplant. He told me because Marky had three surgeries already, his body had built up several antibodies. The more antibodies you have, the harder it is to find a matching organ. However, it was still possible. It was not out of the ordinary for a patient in his condition to get a heart transplant.

The harsh reality was that the only way Marky could get a heart transplant was if someone else were to die. I thought about that for a few seconds, taking in the seriousness of the matter. I cringed at the idea of someone else dying in order to give my son a heart so he could live. The tears swelled up in my eyes as I looked down at the square tile floor. I could hear a pin drop. The hum of the fluorescent lights overhead was now pronounced in my hearing. It felt like a golf ball was lodged in my throat as my mind was flooded with emotions of sadness and grief.

I lifted my head with tears streaming down my cheeks and asked the doctor, "What if I just donated my heart to Marky? Could I volunteer to be his heart donor?"

The doctor smiled at me and gently answered, "No, you cannot volunteer to do that because that would mean ending your life, and that is illegal."

I figured he would say something like that because I had never heard of someone doing that. However, I loved my son with all my heart, so much that I was willing to give up my life so that he could have a fuller and longer life. It broke my heart that I could do nothing more to give him life. I took him to all his doctor's appointments. I followed all the doctor's instructions and gave him his prescribed medicines at the proper times. I became a stay-at-home/work-from-home mom so I could really dedicate myself to taking care of him and his little sister. But at this point, my hands were tied. I realized I had come to the end of my strength, the end of my ability, the end of my power. I had to completely lean on my Heavenly Father for wisdom, knowledge, and healing for my son. I was weak and didn't know what else I could do but pray. I threw myself on the altar of prayer.

I am reminded of when the Apostle Paul talked about the thorn in his flesh. He had an area of weakness that he learned to live with.

But he said to me, "My grace is sufficient for you,
for my power is made perfect in weakness."
Therefore, I will boast all the more gladly about my weaknesses,
so that Christ's power may rest on me.

That is why, for Christ's sake, I delight in weaknesses, in insults, in hardships, in persecutions, in difficulties. For when I am weak, then I am strong.
—2 Corinthians 12: 9-10 (NIV)

Holidays had now become a confusing dichotomy. For me, holiday times were meant for making memories with family and friends, expressing love, and being kind to others. It was very conflicting to be hopeful for a new heart for Marky when it came at the cost of another family's loss. So we started praying for the family of the one who would provide a heart. And then we waited and waited for the next holiday...

Challenge:

1. What are you waiting on God to do in your life? Do you feel like He's taking too long? What is God trying to teach you while you wait?

2. Don't give up on God. It's time to P.U.S.H.— Pray Until Something Happens.

Prayer Focus: Lord, I pray that You grant us the serenity to accept the things we cannot change, courage to change the things we can, and wisdom to know the difference.

CHAPTER 8

Taking Pleasure in the Simple Things

A cheerful heart is good medicine,
but a crushed spirit dries up the bones.
—Proverbs 17:22 (NIV)

I'll never forget one day the previous year when Marky was five, his best friend Kofi came to our house for a playdate. His mom, Lisa, and I stood in the foyer greeting each other. Our sons were so excited to see one another, they hugged and jumped up and down. They overheard Lisa telling me she would be back to pick up Kofi in about two hours. Kofi's head dropped, and he looked sad at the thought that their playtime was only for a short while. Marky consoled Kofi with a hand on his shoulder and said, "Don't worry about it. Let's just have fun with the time we have. We can still have fun." Kofi slowly began to lift his head up, cracked a grin and off they went to play dress up as Spider-Man and Batman. Lisa and I just looked at each other in awe of what happened. The bond our five-year-old sons had was genuine and pure.

Looking back on it now, I realized how profound Marky's comment was. "Let's just have fun with the time we have." Even though he was so young, he knew the value of time. He wanted to focus on and enjoy the good times of his life. He didn't want to dwell on the negative things in his life. Marky knew he had a heart condition, but he didn't allow it to consume his thoughts.

That seemed like so long ago now. Now Marky was back in the hospital confined to this cardiac unit floor while facing this life-threatening illness. I decided to follow Marky's example and paused to take inventory of what was good in my life. Since my family was not living under one roof for long periods of time, I especially cherished the times when the four of us were together in one room, able to enjoy each other's company. I treasured playing a simple game of Uno cards or Monopoly Jr. I cracked up laughing when Marky would hide a rubber mouse around his hospital room to try to scare the nurses or the custodian. Even in the midst of this gut-wrenching storm, I could allow myself to experience joy and to take pleasure in the little blessings along the way.

The enemy wants us to feel defeated. He strives to get us to dwell on our problems and get depressed. When we allow that to happen, then it robs us of our joy. Don't let him steal your joy. Remember the following scriptures:

The joy of the Lord is your strength.
—Nehemiah 8:10 (NKJV)

The thief does not come except to steal, and to kill, and to destroy.
I have come that they may have life,
and that they may have it more abundantly.
—John 10:10 (NKJV)

Here is another blog post I wrote while we were in the hospital awaiting Marky's new heart.

March 5, 2007

I didn't realize it's been almost a week since I updated Marky's journal. So much has happened since then. Marky is getting up and walking around on his own now; he is even pulling his own medicine pole (a pole on wheels that holds his medication and feeding pumps). I just stood in awe, watching him get around and choosing where he wanted to sit in the playroom. While his sister and cousin were visiting over the weekend, he joined them in the play area and was able to reach down and pick up toys and play pretend with them. He looks so much happier as he gains a little more independence each week. He is talking better and is expanding his list of spelling words. He is no longer constipated either. Thank God he's been delivered. His PT/INR (prothrombin/international normalized ratio) level is increasing, but he still has to get the two anticoagulation injections every day until he's at a therapeutic level. I'm praying that it will be high enough when he is retested on Wednesday.

We have been overwhelmed by the generosity of people who care— our family, friends, neighbors, church members, coworkers, and people who we have never met. We have been blessed tremendously. One of Marky's friends did a fundraiser at her mother's job and raised money to help offset the unexpected expenses regarding Marky's hospitalization. Just last week, Marky's elementary school donated 125 books in Marky's honor to the Cardiac Care Unit at CHOP. Over 1300 books were also donated to the rest of CHOP and DuPont Hospital for Children. What a blessing! The school principal, Dr. Denise King, and guidance counselor, Mrs. Jeanene Stefanski, hand-delivered the books to the Cardiac Unit and visited Marky on Thursday. He was pleasantly surprised and enjoyed their visit.

Last night my husband and I silently watched Marky and Naomi interact with each other. We were so grateful to God that Marky was able to pick out which video game he wanted to play, get the cd out of the case, put it in the video system and then worked the controllers. I was about to jump out of my skin when he asked to go to the sink so he could stand to wash his hands and brush his own teeth. He is able to feed himself and tell us when he needs to use the bathroom. (His former PT and OT therapists from duPont Hospital would be so proud of him.) After all the trauma I've seen him go through and (other patients like him), I take pleasure in the simple things in life. Years ago, I used to be unsatisfied with the idea of being a stay-at-home mom, but you know what? I love being a mom, and I love taking care of my family. Just to see my son be able to do all these things and for the four of us to sit in the same room and enjoy a movie together is enough for me. I don't focus so much on the bad things in life anymore; I focus on what is good in my life. I told my husband that our family motto should be "Live, Laugh, and Love." And that is what we are going to do for the rest of our lives.

I love you all and will keep you posted,
Dynita

Let us take a page from Marky's life and think on things that are positive and bring life. Yes, into everyone's life, some rain will fall. But have hope, the sun will shine again. Let's take advantage of our good days. Cherish the times we have with our family, friends, neighbors, and even coworkers. Make memories that will last a lifetime.

Pray without ceasing, in everything give thanks;
for this is the will of God in Christ Jesus for you.
—1 Thessalonians 5:17-18 (NKJV)

Challenge:

1. Get a journal and list three to five things you are thankful to God for, despite the difficult situation you might find yourself in. Try to do this every day or on a regular basis.

2. Practice having an attitude of gratitude. Let your other family members hear you giving thanks for the little things. Ex. Give thanks that it's raining today because the rain is nourishing the earth and helping the flowers, grass, and trees to grow.

3. Do you notice anything different about your mood and your mindset after doing this exercise?

Prayer Focus: God, I thank You for helping me to live with gratitude, joy, and purpose. No matter what I am going through, I will find something to give You thanks for.

CHAPTER 9

Holding Onto My Faith

Be joyful in hope, patient in affliction, faithful in prayer.
—Romans 12:12 (NIV)

Marky's hospital stay continued into the third month. We were taking it one day at a time. Marky persevered through the ups and downs in his health. He tried so hard to cling onto just being a kid, but sometimes he just didn't feel well. Mark and I worked hard to stay positive and fight against any negative thoughts that would try to enter our minds. We encouraged Marky as much as we could, and we did our best to make the most of the times we spent together.

Children's Hospital of Philadelphia did a great job of meeting the needs of its long-term patients. They offered a full range of therapies to Marky. In addition to school and physical therapy, Marky enjoyed music and art therapy. He could draw or paint whatever he wanted. And the music teacher showed him how to make various sounds and music on the keyboard. He most enjoyed the visits from the pets. The dogs would sit with him in his recliner chair and tickle his nose when they licked his face. Marky would let out a loud belly laugh. Petting the dogs on their backs proved to be both exciting and calming at the same time for Marky. This helped to take his mind off his sickness. Not only did this array of therapies help the patients to feel better, but it also helped the caretakers recharge to face another day on the journey.

Here are some blog posts which chronicles our continued journey with Marky for the next four weeks.

March 10, 2007, 1:34 a.m.

Another Good Week

Marky did really well this week. He no longer needs the two injections a day since his INR is back in the normal range. Yeah! His dad gave him a haircut too. And two other patients received their heart transplants in the last two weeks. They are doing well. We are on a roll around here.

Unfortunately, Marky had a traumatic event on Wednesday when he had to get his feeding tube replaced (in the nose). It was not fun at all, but he eventually settled down. However, on Thursday evening, he started coughing a lot and he fell asleep early. He was up for much of the night vomiting, and the feeding tube was coughed out. Ugh! Since he had such a rough night, he tried to take it easy on Friday. But he had to endure getting an echocardiogram and the feeding tube replaced again. This time we used a more effective sedative to help him get through it. Later he developed a fever of 102, which raised his heart rate and affected his breathing. After getting Tylenol, the fever went down (and the heart rate), but the staff is keeping a close eye on him and hoping that it's only a twenty-four-hour bug. He's getting oxygen supplements, and they are doing blood tests to rule out any infections. Please pray that Marky will overcome this "bug" quickly and that he can get some good sleep. If it were to progress any further, he could be taken off the transplant list. But I know that God is in control, and I'm trusting that He will bring Marky through this too. Enjoy the updated photos and have a good weekend.

Love,
Dynita

March 13, 2007, 12:32 a.m.

Rejoice in the Lord Always

Thank you for your prayers. We think Marky is over the "bug" he caught last week. I think it was passed throughout some of the patients in the Cardiac unit. For the most part, he feels better but is left with another nasty cough. Part of the reason for the cough is that it is just a common symptom of congestive heart failure. At least today he was able to do all his activities and spend some time in the playroom. His INR level has been erratic. It was as high as fourteen on Saturday and has since dropped to 1.5. The normal range is 2.5–3.5. If the level is above the range, it means his blood is too thin and will not clot fast enough. Vice versa if the level is below the range, he could be at risk for a blood clot. So now he has to get the two anticoagulant injections a day until it's back in the normal range. We don't know what is causing the sudden changes, but the doctors are keeping a close eye on it. He is still on the transplant list, but the reality is that when a heart becomes available to Marky, his INR level could have an impact on whether the doctors would perform the surgery because of the potential risk of bleeding or blood clots. So I am praying that God gives us the wisdom on how to get him into the normal range and maintain it so that he can be ready when the right heart comes.

On Tuesday, Marky is heading back to the dentist for a teeth cleaning. Please keep him in prayer because something as simple as a visit to the dentist is not so easy for Marky. He has a very difficult time sitting reclined in the dental chair. I suspect that he has difficulty breathing in certain positions, but it could also be anxiety. So I'm praying that he will have great success in this area.

I was sad to hear that two babies in the CICU had passed away last week. This is a difficult reality that we face week after week. I am just grateful for another day of life for Marky. This is the day that the Lord has made. I will rejoice and be glad in it. Psalm 118:24

God Bless You All,
Dynita

March 16, 2007, 4:50 p.m.

Field Trip

Guess where Marky went yesterday? He Went Outside! Besides the day he was transferred from DuPont Hospital to CHOP, this was the first day he was able to go outside. He and one other patient, Ricky, enjoyed blowing bubbles and shooting Spider-Man webs. It was exciting for them. Check out the pictures in the photo gallery.

Overall, Marky had a good week. He made out fine at the dentist getting his teeth cleaned. His PT/INR level is back in the normal range, so no more extra injections. And the symptoms from the "bug" he caught last week are gone. Yeah! He is walking and riding his tricycle faster, and his speech is also improving.

We have nothing but praises and thanks to the almighty God who continues to sustain Marky's life and give us peace.

Be Blessed,
Dynita

P.S. Marky's favorite stuffed animal dog, Yoey, has been missing since last Tuesday. We think he was accidentally put in the soiled linen bin, which gets sent all the way to Maryland for cleaning. It broke my heart to hear him cry himself to sleep for almost an hour. Please pray for Yoey's safe return to Marky. He has been with Marky through all his ups and downs for the last four years. Thank you.

March 23, 2007, 2:54 p.m.

Hello,

Marky has had another great week! Overall, he is feeling pretty good and hasn't had any major problems. He's starting to get over the possibility that his stuffed animal dog Yoey may never return. This may be God's way of teaching him that we can only truly depend on the Lord to be with us at all times. It's never too early to learn these truths, however painful they may be.

When I returned to the hospital yesterday, I was overjoyed to see how much progress Marky is making. He can tie his shoelaces by himself, his writing has improved, and he is handling scissors much better than before. He is also able to bend down to pick up objects off the floor. These are goals we've been working on for some time now, and he is slowly but surely meeting them.

Marky enjoyed a music band who entertained the patients on Tuesday, and then Wednesday, there was a Mardi Gras celebration. Thursday, they enjoyed a fruit demonstration from two of the hospital chefs. This is an effort to get the patients eating more. They tasted all kinds of fruit.

We'll keep you posted on his progress, and we continue praying for the heart donor.

Dynita

March 27, 2007, 3:59 a.m.

A Rough Weekend

Just want to solicit your prayers once more. Marky started coughing a lot over the weekend, and at about 2:30 this morning, he was moved to the CICU. We're not sure if it's a cold, a virus, or reactive airways, but the doctors want to take precautions and watch him closer to prevent him from getting sicker. His medications have been adjusted to help him with his breathing, including some supplemental oxygen at night. He also had to get a blood transfusion on Sunday, and Monday afternoon, he had an echocardiogram. He's had several x-rays, and they've all showed no infection. However, the truth of the matter is that they can't see all of Marky's lungs because his heart is so big. Lord, please reveal things to us that the natural eyes cannot see. Please pray for Marky's quick stabilization and for wisdom for the doctors to give him the right treatments.

The transplant doctor said Marky had several heart donor offers; however, they weren't great matches. Since Marky has been doing so well, we've had the luxury of waiting for a better heart. Let's pray that Marky will be able to continue to wait for the perfect heart.

I came home last night but will be heading back to the hospital as soon as day breaks. Thank you for your prayers.

Dynita

P.S. I just got an update. He has a cold. Thank goodness we know what it is. He is doing ok, even though he's not getting much sleep because he's uncomfortable.

March 27, 2007, 11:14 p.m.

Back in the Step-Down Unit

Thank you so much for your fervent prayers. The Lord was certainly watching over Marky. He is doing much better since last night. It was later determined that he has RSV, a contagious respiratory virus, which seems to be going around the cardiac unit. Well, it's not so great that he has RSV, but at least the doctors know what it is and how to treat it. They were concerned that his heart was getting progressively worse, but thank goodness, this is not the case. Marky was able to participate in all his therapies today, and he even ate some of his dinner, BBQ chicken. He was doing well enough to go back to the regular Cardiac Care Unit, known as step-down, around 4:30 p.m. Please pray that Marky's symptoms (wheezing, coughing, sneezing, restlessness) will cease and that he will recover from this quickly.

I am just so thankful that he is doing so much better. The last two nights, I received a call from Marky's nurse. And each time, my heart raced with different emotions; excitement because this could be the call about a donor heart and then fear if it was bad news (all within a split second). But God is faithful, and I know He won't put more on me than I can handle, so I just continue to trust Him and look to Him for the strength I need to ride this roller coaster ride with Marky. Be blessed and know that God is with you every step of the way.

Love,
Dynita

March 28, 2007, 5:27 p.m.

Marky is having a good day even though he doesn't feel that well. Apparently, there is an outbreak of RSV among some of the cardiac patients. But the good news is that Marky is back in his original room again (yes, we moved again).

Blessings,
Dynita

March 29, 2007, 10:37 a.m.

Fever Broke

Last night Marky spiked a fever of about 102 degrees F. He was in and out of sleep and looked really bad. After he received Motrin, the fever broke. He looks and sounds much better this morning. He's having school now. Even though Marky is contained in his room until the RSV virus clears, the teacher and therapists come into his room as long as he's feeling up to it. Since the RSV virus is widespread (throughout the hospital), the playroom and family lounges in the cardiac unit are closed for a thorough cleaning, and the patients cannot have any visitors until further notice. The Hospital is working along with the Infectious Control department to take measures to contain the virus and keep it from getting worse. Marky is still coughing a lot and having trouble with his breathing. I'm praying that he's seen the worst of it already and will get better soon. I'll keep in touch.

Dynita

March 30, 2007, 5:23 p.m.

Marky Still Under the Weather

For the last two days, Marky has not been feeling well. The fever still comes and goes. After taking a blood culture yesterday, it was discovered that Marky has an infection in the PIC line (this is the line that his IV medications run through and blood can be drawn from). He is getting some antibiotics for the infection and steroids to treat the reactive airways brought on by the RSV. He is really in a bad way, but I've seen him in much worse conditions, so relatively speaking, he is still doing okay. He's been in and out of sleep all day and not able to stay awake long enough to do his therapies. Although he looks exhausted, he is determined to sit in his comfortable recliner until bedtime again.

One thing I've learned from all this is that even though Marky is small in stature, he is really a strong boy. Even after all the blood draws, the nasty tasting medicines three or four times a day, the vomiting, the dressing changes, the tubes and wires, the constant prodding and poking, somehow he still rebounds with a smile and joyful attitude. He is showing us that the joy of the Lord is really his strength, and he will not let this sickness or any other obstacle brought on by Satan to steal his joy.

The thief does not come except to steal, and to kill, and to destroy, but I (Jesus) have come that you might have life and have it more abundantly. John 10:10

This is the promise that we are standing on. We will not waiver. We will not bend. We will stand still and know that Marky's deliverance is on the way. Yesterday I asked Marky if he wanted me to pray with him. He said yes. I asked him if the Lord were to come get him today, would he be ready. He said yes. And then I asked him if he wanted to keep fighting for his life or was he ready to give up. He clearly stated that he did not want to give up. He has plans to grow up and become a husband and father one day. So I prayed with Marky before I left for the night. And we declared that ***He Is Healed, in Jesus' Name.***

Be Blessed,
Dynita

March 30, 2007, 9:08 p.m.

Moved to CICU

Hi all. Just wanted you to know that Marky is temporarily in the CICU tonight for close observation. He is about the same that he was earlier today, but they just want to monitor him closely overnight to prevent him from getting any worse. He's having a tough time shaking this RSV. But I know there is nothing too hard for God to solve. Prayerfully, he will be well enough to go back to the step-down unit by tomorrow.

Dynita

March 31, 2007, 8:53 a.m.

CICU Update

It sounds like Marky will be in the CICU for the weekend. The doctors decided to put in an arterial line (main vein in the wrist) to measure his gases, which so far have been good. They also talked about possibly needing to do another blood transfusion and putting him back on the ventilator, but for now, he's on the CPAP (similar to the BiPap). Once he got used to it, he was able to get better rest overnight. His INR level is very high—12.9, so they are trying to get that down to the normal range.

There is some elevation in the output of his liver, which indicates that the heart is having a harder time doing its job. And his kidney output is low because he must be holding on to some fluid. His swollen hands, feet, and eyelids are also indicators of this. So they are treating that by giving him more diuretics. He could not eat anything as of last night (not that he wanted to), so they are giving him IV nutrition. I should have another report by this afternoon. I'm expecting a positive report.

Holding on,
Dynita

April 1, 2007, 7:36 p.m.

The Hand of God

The doctors are still trying to clear the blood infection from the PIC line with antibiotics, but if this doesn't happen by tomorrow morning, they will have to remove it and the arterial line. Then another line will be placed in the groin so his medications can be run through it. To do this, Mark will need to lie flat, which is a big ordeal for him. Therefore, they will have to use some type of sedation, which comes with some risks. He already received one new IV today, and he may need another one put in tomorrow. A third blood transfusion was also given today. He is still on the CPAP machine, which assists him with breathing. They may start weaning him from it tomorrow. His eyelids are less puffy, but his hands and feet are sore because they are so swollen. Even his right arm swelled up but has since started to go down. He wants to eat and drink, but he is still restricted from taking anything by mouth for now. One other thing is that his INR level is still high; it's at fifteen. The doctors want to wait for it to come down on its own instead of giving him vitamin K like before. The vitamin K brought it down too low before, and then he was at risk for blood clots. He definitely doesn't need that. And I also found out that Marky was deactivated from the transplant list earlier last week. Once he is over the infection, off the CPAP, and is stronger, he can be reactivated.

Even with all these issues, we can see the Hand of God moving on Marky's behalf. He is more talkative, and his feisty attitude is returning. (Most of you don't know that side of Marky. He usually saves that for his sister and the medical staff.) Even though he is complaining a lot about the mask on his face (our DuPont friends know how much he loooooves the BiPap contraption) and the soreness of his body, this is a great indicator that he has more energy. He stayed awake for almost nine hours, so he didn't need to take the frequent naps during the day. He is getting better rest at night. And he even played a game of Uno cards with me. Oh, how I treasure those moments.

Tomorrow will be a busy day for Marky, so please pray for continued improvements and that there won't be any complications with the procedure he may need to undergo.

Thank you for your encouragement,

Dynita

P.S. I just found out that his INR is back down to 3.5, which is in the normal range. Yeah!

April 4, 2007, 2:20 p.m.

Doing Better

Marky is doing better. He's not out of the woods yet, but he's definitely doing better. He is still in the CICU. He's been having some PVCs (extra heartbeats) off and on, so please continue to pray that he doesn't experience any dangerous rhythms that could cause serious problems. Pray for continued strength for his heart function and all his other organs as well. The PIC line was still infected, so it was removed yesterday. The doctors are trying to allow him more time for the blood to clear the infection before putting in the new PIC line. This is scheduled for tomorrow. Please pray that the infection will cease and that he will get over the RSV. All his medications are temporarily running through peripheral IVs. He's still coughing but a lot less. All the swelling in his body went down. He is able to be off the CPAP machine for longer times during the day. He mostly uses it while he's sleeping. This morning his nurse gave him the good news that he could eat today. As he tried to open his sleepy eyes, he smiled. That was the first real smile we've seen in a long time.

He started off with some cereal and apple juice. He said, "This apple juice sure is good." He had the doctors cracking up yesterday when he asked repeatedly when he could have some water or ice chips. They said soon. Then he talked about eating. He said, "Do I have to eat in my bed?" The doctor said, "Well, where do you want to eat? In the cafeteria?" Marky's left eyebrow went up as if he were thinking, "That's not a bad idea." The other doctor said, "Well, where else do you want to eat?" "Applebee's.," he said as a matter of factly. He caught us all off guard with that one. Applebee's is his favorite restaurant.

It reminded me of a time back in November, when just Marky and I went out on a lunch date. He selected Applebee's, of course. We had a good time. He ordered his usual, chicken fingers with French fries and a Sprite. We talked a lot about the play we recently saw at our church, "Heaven's Gates, Hell's Flames." I used it as a forum to talk about the importance of being saved. He was so captivated by the play that he wants to be in the next one.

This is one of his motivators for getting well soon. For now, he is getting his much-needed rest to reach that goal.

Be Blessed,
Dynita

P.S. Hug your loved one a little longer next time.

Let me take this moment to interject with a significant occurrence in Marky's life as a result of several conversations I had with him prior to him getting really sick. Marky publicly accepted the Lord into his heart on December 25th 2005 at church. His Uncle Darryl preached the message that Christmas Sunday morning. While Pastor Aubrey gave the invitation to Christ, Marky told me he was ready to give his life to the Lord in front of the church. I stood him up on the red cushioned chairs so the pastor could see his short stature over the congregation. Pastor Aubrey invited him to come to the altar. Mark Sr. and I escorted our son to the front of the church. Reverend Darryl Washington was ecstatic that his nephew had made such a wise choice at only five years of age. Darryl kneeled down on one knee to be on Marky's level and led him in the prayer of salvation. We all rejoiced in that precious moment.

Later that night in bed, I reminisced with my husband about the day's events. I found myself crying while thinking about what the future held for my son. I was thrilled that he publicly professed his love for Christ on that day; however, my tears were not of joy this time. They flowed with a heaviness and with a hint of sorrow. I sensed that something was coming in his future. I didn't know what, but I continued to put my trust in God and live by faith that He would take care of me and my family. I could find peace knowing that Marky's soul was ready, no matter what happened next.

April 5, 2007, 7:19 p.m.
Back on the Ventilator

Marky spiked a fever this afternoon of about 104 degrees. He was shivering and had difficulty breathing. The doctors put him back on the ventilator to take some strain off his heart. He is sedated and resting now. He still is testing positive for an infection in the blood. They are wondering if the infection reached the heart or prosthetic heart valve. We don't know for sure. The fevers may reoccur. Please pray for Marky's complete healing. He was wide awake before they sedated him, and he prayed along with his Uncle Darryl for Jesus to heal him. And we know He will.

Dynita

April 5, 2007, 9:21 p.m.

ECMO Machine

As they were putting in a new PIC line, Marky lost blood pressure. He started having arrhythmias. They are doing chest compressions as we speak. We are waiting for the Chief Surgeon to come in and put him up on the ECMO machine, which is an artificial heart-lung machine similar to the bypass machines used in open heart surgery. This will do the work of the heart and lungs and give his organs a break. They reactivated him on the transplant list. Although it's not optimal conditions, the doctors will consider good heart offers at this time. Only God can help Marky get through this. Big Mark, my mom, and sister are here with us. Please keep on praying.

Dynita

April 6, 2007, 1:39 a.m.

Somewhat Stable

Marky is on ECMO now. His heart and lungs are resting while the machine does the work for him. He is somewhat stable. Please pray for the blood infection to clear and that a very good heart offer comes soon for him. Please pray that his brain, kidneys, liver, and other organs will continue to function properly. And pray for the doctors, nurses, and everyone who comes in contact with Marky. And please pray for my husband and me.

As the scripture says: Though I walk through the valley of the shadow of death, I will fear no evil because You are with me.

Standing on the promises of God,
Dynita

April 6, 2007, 5:08 p.m.

Stable But in Critical Condition

Marky has done well on the ECMO machine so far. Since the machine works better with gravity, they had to elevate his bed with two extra mattresses. So we have to stand on stools to see him on the bed. The surgeon said he cannot be transplanted with an active infection, so he was deactivated from the transplant list this morning until the blood infection is cleared. They are trying different antibiotics to fight it. So far, the blood culture from today is negative; we are praying that nothing grows on it over the next forty-eight hours.

The ***good news*** *is that Marky wakes up and responds appropriately to our questions by shaking his head yes and no. He is able to wiggle his toes and fingers on command. Clearly, he can hear* *us, even though he can't really focus his eyes on us yet. So neurologically, he seems to be okay.*

Another good sign is that even though his heart is resting, it is still pumping on its own. (However, he is having a lot of extra heartbeats, so please pray for a normal heart rhythm.) The goal is to give his heart and lungs time to rest before weaning him off the ECMO machine. It is important that he come off the machine soon because having another foreign object in the body can present another source of infection. And plus after a few weeks, the other organs could start giving out. So we are prayerful that he will be strong enough to be weaned off it soon.

No matter what it looks like, we still believe that ***Marky's body is healed****. We are standing on God's promises and are claiming the victory for our son.*

April 7, 2007, 11:40 a.m.

Prayer Requests

Marky had a good night overall. He is having fewer extra heartbeats. He continues to be stable; however, the infection is still in his blood and he has not been urinating enough. Here is what we are praying for today:

Father, I thank you that:

- *Marky's blood is cleared from all infection, and he is reactivated onto the heart transplant list.*
- *His kidneys, liver, lungs, brain, spleen, intestines, pancreas, and all other organs are working properly.*
- *His heart is strong enough to pump the blood through the body so that he can get off the ECMO machine.*

- *You are supplying a new heart for Marky, and he is made whole.*

Thank you for your continual prayers. They are helping to keep us strong at such a difficult time. We can be reached in Marky's room during the days and evenings or at nights and mornings at the Ronald McDonald House. At this time, we are limiting the visitations to immediate family members and the clergy.

Yours in Christ,
Dynita & Mark

April 8, 2007, 11:18 p.m.

Happy Resurrection Sunday!

We rejoiced today that Jesus Christ is alive. The same resurrection power that raised Jesus from the dead is the same power that is raising Marky from his sick bed. There have been sooooo many prayers going up for Marky, and we are seeing the results of the prayers every day. Today Marky made several improvements. The ECMO Specialist on duty last night decided that Marky needed to be raised up higher for the machine to work at its best. So they added two more mattresses to his bed; now Marky is five mattresses high. We have to stand on a chair just to see him. His blood pressure improved, his kidneys started working better, and the swelling in his face started to go down. The blood cultures have been negative since Friday, which is a good indication that the infection is gone. We won't know for sure until tomorrow. When my husband and I returned from church today, they turned off the sedative to allow Marky to wake up so they could check his neurological status. Eventually, he did wake up and was able to move his arms and legs on command and nod his head. He even opened his puffy eyes briefly.

He told us he was in pain, so they put him back on the sedative so he could be comfortable again. It hurt me to see that he was in so much pain, but it was reassuring to know that he could respond appropriately. We believe Marky is turning a corner and that he will continue to improve. Please continue to pray for the following:

- *Marky's liver and kidney functions*
- *Blood infection and the RSV virus completely cleared*
- *Staying free of infections and fevers*
- *Wisdom as to when he can come off the ECMO machine, better heart function*
- *Wisdom to know when he should be reactivated on the transplant list*
- *The perfect heart for Marky and for the donor family*

Thank you for standing with us during this difficult season of our lives. We are truly blessed to have you all by our side.

God bless you all,
Dynita

April 9, 2007, 11:35 a.m.

Coming Off ECMO Today

Marky had another stable night. The blood cultures are still negative since Friday, so there is no sign of infection. Praise God! The doctors have lowered the circuit settings of the ECMO machine, and so far, Marky is doing fine. They even tested him off the machine for a few minutes, and he was stable. They feel that now is a good time to take him off the machine; his heart and lungs seem to be ready to do the work on their own. Plus, they feel that his kidneys and liver will function better once he's off the machine. So the plan is to take him off the ECMO machine around 2 p.m. today. So please pray specifically that there will be no complications taking him off the machine and that his organs will function properly. Lord, please give the doctors, nurses, therapists, and everyone who comes in contact with him the wisdom on how to handle Marky and his unusual physiology.

I'll keep you updated.

Dynita

April 9, 2007, 4:43 p.m.

Tomorrow Is Miracle Day for Marky

The doctors at CHOP have decided to give Marky another day to rest his heart before removing the ECMO machine. Marky has a unique anatomy, which makes the ECMO machine inadequate to sustain his life while we wait for a donor heart to become available. There are also signs that his kidneys and liver are not tolerating the machine. Therefore, the ECMO machine, which saved his life last week, will be removed tomorrow, and Marky's heart will have to function well enough to support the function of all his internal organs. Then Marky will live and remain in the transplant program. Once the ECMO machine is removed tomorrow, going back on it will not be an option, so tomorrow is "Miracle Day for Marky."

You can help Marky, by praying for:

- *The removal of the ECMO machine without complications*
- *Heart function to be robust and sustaining*

- *Optimal blood pressure*
- *Excellent brain, kidney, liver, and other internal organ function*
- *The absence of any infections or fever*
- *A rapid recovery from the anesthesia*
- *A restoration of strength in his entire body.*
- *A donor heart to become available soon and a successful transplant*

In summary, we need and expect a miracle for Marky tomorrow in Jesus' name!

Thanks,
Mark Sr.

April 11, 2007, 12:57 a.m.

Made It Through Today

Marky came off the ECMO machine around 3:15 p.m. on Tuesday. There were no complications, and his heart is pumping on its own. At one time this evening, his blood pressure started dropping, but they gave him a blood transfusion, among other things, and got it back in an acceptable range. His skin turned an orangey color over the last few days because the liver has not been metabolizing the antibiotics, so we are praying for this to be turned around. He is still on the ventilator and is also on Nitric Oxide, which helps to open up his pulmonary arteries. His body is swollen because of the excess fluid. Marky is under sedation and he looks comfortable. We continue to put his foot splints and knee immobilizers on him to prevent foot drop and his tendons and hamstrings from getting tight. He is getting excellent care around the clock. Since I didn't get much rest last night, I figured I might as well be at the hospital and hopefully get more sleep. So Mark and I are spending the night in Marky's room tonight. We are still praying specifically for the following:

- *Heart function to be robust and sustaining*
- *Optimal blood pressure*
- *Excellent brain, kidney, liver, and other internal organ function (pray for lots of pee and for his liver to reduce in size)*
- *Nose bleeds to stop*
- *The absence of any infections or fever*
- *A rapid recovery from the anesthesia*
- *A restoration of strength in his entire body.*
- *To get back on the transplant list, the right donor heart to become available soon and a successful transplant*

There were some who didn't think he would make it through coming off the machine. But he beat the odds, and we are grateful that he made it through this day. This is a miracle in itself. We are still standing on God's Word and claim healing, restoration, and wholeness for Marky. We are so grateful for all the prayers going up for him.

Love,
Dynita & Mark

April 11, 2007, 12:15 p.m.

Dear Family & Friends,

Marky made it through the night; however, his kidneys and liver are shutting down, and the doctors are giving him twelve to twenty-four hours to live. We certainly are still praying for another miracle, but if God says otherwise, we know that Marky will be with the Lord. Please continue to pray for him and our strength.

Love to you all,
Dynita & Mark Sr.

Challenge:

1. What do you pray when the doctor says there is nothing more they can do?
2. Is it too late for God to turn things around? What miracles have you seen or heard about when the worse situation turned around and surprised even the medical professionals?
3. How do you prepare yourself and your loved one for the ultimate transition?

Prayer Focus: Heavenly Father, our Creator, let Your will be done in our lives. I know You are Jehovah Rophe, the healer. I will trust in You for the final say.

CHAPTER 10

Strong Enough to Let Go

To everything there is a season, a time for every purpose under heaven.
A time to be born, and a time to die...
—Ecclesiastes 3:1-2a (NKJV)

After the doctor gave me the dismal news that Marky only had twelve to twenty-four hours to live, I quickly found my husband, who was out in the lounge making phone calls to the family. Mark's mom and our daughter, Naomi, were visiting family during spring break in Lawrenceville, Georgia, just outside of Atlanta. We had held them off from returning early because we were expecting Marky to make a turnaround and pull through as he had done so many times before. But at this point, I told Mark to call them and ask them to get on the next flight to Philadelphia. We contacted our other family and close friends and told them to come to the hospital to be with us. Visitors started rolling in to see Marky. Even Marky's longtime cardiologist, Dr. Anisman, paid a visit to express his concern and affection for Marky, one of his most memorable patients who made him smile. One by one, the people were showing up, some to say their goodbyes and others to pray for a miracle of healing. My parents, sister, brother, and future sister-in-law were there to give their support. As each visitor came to the door, they were instructed to put on a yellow gown over their clothes. We even played the

DVDs and CDs made by his school classmates, teachers, and the Koinonia Kids choir at our church. We put the speaker right next to Marky's ear so he could hear all the well wishes from his friends from church and school. We stood around his bed and continued praying for Marky and singing songs to him. Although he was sedated, the nurses told us that he could hear our voices. But for the most part, his body laid still. My husband and I were still praying in our hearts for a miracle healing to take place. As long as there was breath in his body, we did not give up hope.

My dear mother-in-law, affectionately known as Grandmom Rita to my kids, desperately wanted to get back to Philly so she could see Marky for what could be the last time. Although she was a woman of great faith, she could hear it in our voices, and she could read between the lines of our blog posts that Marky's condition was worsening. After hearing from Mark that Tuesday morning, she called the airline right away and bought two one-way tickets for a two o'clock flight so that she and Naomi could return immediately. She was already partially packed anyway, so it didn't take long to get their things together. My brother-in-law Greg knew he needed to put the pedal to the metal because it normally takes fifty minutes to get to the airport. Putting his NASCAR-like motor skills into motion, zig-zagging through the traffic and zipping down I-85 south, Greg got them to the airport just in time for the flight.

Just outside the entrance, Mom approached the airport porter to get their bags checked in for the flight. The man politely told her that they could no longer accept bags for that flight because the plane was going to take off in minutes. She pleaded with the man and told him, "I've got to get on this plane to go see my grandson, who is gravely ill and about to die." He saw the sorrow in her eyes and said, "I hope I don't get fired for this," and he took their bags. The automatic door entrance opened, and they hurried inside to find the signs that would lead them to the security line. Mom Rita gripped Mimi's little hand tightly, and they ran down the corridor to find their way.

As they were coming up on the security line, her eyes got big and her jaw dropped. They joined the end of the line, but she could see the line was so long it wrapped around the security ropes several times. She was so dismayed. She told the lady behind her that they were in a huge rush home because her grandson Marky was soon to pass away. The lady told her, "Well then go straight up to the front of the line and tell them that it's an emergency! They'll let you through." Mom Rita followed her suggestion, and they bolted past the people in line, ignoring any crazy looks and stares from the other passengers. They reached the front of the line nearly in tears and explained the situation to the security check staff, and they let her through immediately. With Mimi holding onto grandmom's hand tightly, they ran swiftly through a packed Hartsfield International Airport to find the terminal. Her four-year-old little legs had to move fast enough to keep up. They were both out of breath when they arrived at the terminal; however, Mom Rita soon realized they were in the wrong section of the airport. "Oh no," she gasped. Feeling anxious and nervous about possibly missing the plane, she looked around frantically and decided to go through a side door, which led to a small lounge area for the employees. She quickly told them she needed help finding the right terminal, and one of the employees graciously showed her the way. Thank God it was only a few more steps away, and they were in the right place.

By then, the door of the gate should have been closed. Nevertheless, when they arrived at the gate, passengers were still getting their boarding passes scanned. Wasting no time, they grabbed their carry-on bags and hastily jumped in line, got their boarding passes scanned, and entered the boarding ramp to head to the plane. Yes!

They had made it onto the plane before the gate closed. After finding their seats and getting settled in, Mom Rita asked the flight attendant why the plane hadn't left yet. He said, "I don't know, but we were supposed to depart forty-five minutes ago. For some strange reason, there was a delay." Mom Rita relaxed back in her seat and cracked a smile, quietly thanking God. She truly believed that God, in His infinite wisdom and power, had delayed the plane so that she and Naomi could catch that flight. They were on their way to join the rest of the family and be with Marky.

It was about 5:25 p.m., and we could see on the patient monitor that Marky's blood pressure was dropping quickly. The doctors and nursing staff were working hard around the clock, giving him all kinds of supplements and increasing the medications to keep his heart pumping while more family members were arriving to see Marky. I called Mark's cell phone to see where he was. He and my dad had just returned to the hospital after picking up his mother and Naomi from the airport. Within minutes, Mom Rita and Naomi showed up in the CICU wearing their matching yellow sweat suits. The cardiologist, Dr. Chitra Ravishankar, told Mom Rita, "Hurry up on inside because he's not going to last much longer. He's been waiting for you and his sister to arrive." I reunited with Naomi in the hallway, gave her an embrace, and talked with her about Marky. I explained that Marky was really sick this time, and then Mark & I took her into the room to see him. Normally, Naomi's number one goal when visiting her big brother was to make him smile and laugh. She would put on her silliest act to get some giggles out of him. This was something she treasured and Marky looked forward to. But this time when she walked into the room, she sensed that it was different. She heard the children's music playing softly in the background. She saw that Marky was asleep, and an unusual number of people were in the room praying. Somewhat hiding behind my leg, she was acting shy and, for the first time, at a loss for words. She quietly said hello to Marky and within minutes said goodbye, and then she was taken out to a lounge area to play.

It was becoming increasingly clearer that Marky's heart function was worsening. Once most of the family had arrived to see Marky, my husband and I made the excruciating decision to let him go naturally. We didn't want the process sped up nor prolonged unnecessarily. We told the doctor of our wishes, and they continued to monitor his vital signs. They turned off the overhead monitor so we would not be distracted by it, and they gave us privacy. We could still see the rapid chest movements from his heart pumping, and the ventilator was pretty much doing the breathing for him.

The Lord sent two men of the clergy our way to minister to Marky and our family during this precious time, Reverend Derek Wilson and Pastor Maurice Talley. They led us in prayer and gave exhortations of encouragement and comfort. Pastor Talley was then led to anoint Marky with oil. We had moved hospital rooms so much that I couldn't find our anointing oil, but the cafeteria staff sent some oil up to the room right away. He blessed the oil and instructed everyone in the room to touch the person nearest to them to create an unbroken chain. He was on one side of Marky's bed, and Reverend Derek was on the other side of the bed. My husband was in contact with Pastor Talley, and I was in contact with Mark and so on.

Now I've been in church pretty much all my life, and I've seen people get anointed plenty of times before. I was expecting the typical anointing of oil on the forehead and maybe on the hands. However, Pastor Talley did things differently. He led us in the song "Anointing Fall on Me" by Ron Kenoly. At this point, there was an assembly of thirty-plus people in the room singing, touching, agreeing, and waiting with anticipation of what the Lord was going to do. Pastor Talley proceeded to anoint Marky's entire body with the oil, his face, neck, shoulders, arms, all the way down to his feet. Pastor Derek did the same on the other side of Marky.

Naomi was back in the room by this time and was sitting on the foot of Marky's bed, looking at what was going on. She was playing with his feet, seeking some attention from Marky as she would normally do.

As I was trying to get her to stop messing with him, she asked me, "Did Marky die?"

I whispered to her, "No, not yet."

Her eyes started to water, and she asked again, "Is Marky about to die?"

Sadly, I told her, "Probably so. Soon."

"Is he going to heaven?"

"Yes, he will be in heaven with Jesus soon."

She then began to cry. I realized that she got it. She understood that her big brother was soon to leave us. I hugged her and held her close to me to console her.

"Then can we get a dog?" she blurted out, looking up at me with bloodshot eyes and tears rolling down her face.

I was totally caught off guard by her request. I had to crack a slight grin at the innocent wish from a child who's realized her playmate and best friend was leaving her and she didn't want to spend the rest of her life alone. Without making a big deal, I told her we would discuss it later, but not right now. She buried her face into my hip and cried.

Pastor Talley continued to pray over Marky. I don't remember everything he said word for word, but I do remember him praying to God, "Lord, if it is Your will to heal Marky, we know that You can, and we are open to that even now. But if it is Your will to take Marky to be with You, then we will accept it. Lord, I ask that You let him lay his eyes upon his mother one more time." After he ended the prayer, he told Mark and I not to let anyone besides the medical staff touch Marky's body now because his body was consecrated to the Lord. My husband quickly covered Marky's body with a blanket up to his shoulders. Pastor Talley excused himself and turned around to leave the room so the family could have some space. He started pressing through the crowd of people, and Mark followed behind to thank him for coming.

We continued to hover over Marky's bed, singing and observing his swollen body. Even his eyes were swollen shut. Then suddenly, Marky opened his left eye and looked at me. Everyone in the room gasped, and we started calling out his name. My husband rushed back to his bedside. We both told him how much we loved him and how proud we were of him. The tears were just streaming down our faces as we poured our hearts out to him. I told him not to be afraid because he was going to live with Jesus in heaven and that we would all see him again when it was our turn to come. I assured him that he would be okay; he wouldn't need any more medicines, needles, surgeries, or hospital stays. He would not have any more heart problems or pain.

Although it broke our hearts to let him go, we had to release him to God. He kept his eye open long enough to let us know that he heard our voices and that he was okay. His eye closed, and a tear came down the right side of his face. Shortly thereafter, I saw his shoulders sort of shrug twice. I immediately noticed that the chest movements were less pronounced, and I quickly pulled down the blanket to get a closer look. Then the doctor squeezed through the crowd to get to his bedside and listened to his heart with her stethoscope. She said, "He's gone. His heart stopped. I'm so sorry." We had just watched Marky take his last two breaths.

My sister Monica recalls Naomi said, "Mom, did you see that? Did you see that angel?"

We looked up above Marky, but all I saw were the dark silent monitors and medical equipment that once were filled with vital signs charting his every breath and heartbeat. However, my daughter saw an angelic being, no doubt the one who came to escort her big brother to his new home in heaven. We were in awe.

The room was immediately filled with sobbing and weeping from everyone in the room. We consoled one another with hugs. But I had an odd sense of relief. I was strangely relieved that the long journey of Marky's suffering was over. It's not that I wanted the journey to be over; I didn't. I was certainly prepared and wanted to go the long haul with Marky. But surprisingly, it was okay; it was well with my soul. I gave thanks to God for taking him out of this miserable condition peacefully and that he wasn't alone in those final hours. I belted out the words to the song, "When we all get to heaven, what a day of rejoicing that will be. When we all see Jesus, we will sing and shout the victory." The mourners all joined in with singing, clapping, and praising God, for this is the hope of the Christian life, that we will one day see our Lord and Savior Jesus Christ and our loved ones who also believed.

I think most of us were in disbelief, totally shocked at what had happened. Some of us were still lingering around his bed, hoping and praying that life would return to his body. We thought, *This couldn't be it.* Marky was so strong and had bounced back from dire medical conditions before, and he could do it again. But God had the final say. I can imagine God telling Marky that he had endured enough and had completed his purpose in life. Now it was time to come to his eternal home and enter into his rest. We were so sad but grateful to God that He gave us the opportunity to say goodbye to Marky and to witness the miracle of Marky opening his eye one last time to say goodbye to us. This was Marky's initial homegoing service. What we held at the church six days later was "A Celebration of His Life"—hence the reason why we could lift our hands in praise and adoration to the Lord, totally surrendering ourselves to the will of our Heavenly Father.

Looking back, it was amazing to see how God had orchestrated everything perfectly. My mother-in-law and Naomi flew in from Atlanta just in the nick of time to join the rest of the family and friends. Of all people, the Lord sent Pastor Derek Wilson to be there, whom Marky adored ever since Derek played the role of Jesus in the play "Heaven's Gates, Hell's Flames." His portrayal of Jesus made such a lasting impression on Marky's heart and mind that Marky accepted Christ in his heart at the tender age of five. The Lord also sent Pastor Talley to the hospital. We later remembered that he was one of the first ones who laid hands on me and prayed for Marky when he was still in my womb after we had learned of the dreadful diagnosis of the heart condition. And subsequently, Pastor Talley was the last one who prayed for Marky at the end of his life. We saw miracle after miracle from the time our son was born, up until his last day. We are so grateful to God for lending Marky to us for a short time. He was truly a gift from the Lord.

A well-known quote by Hermann Hesse states, "Some of us think holding on makes us strong, but sometimes it is letting go." I did everything in my power to give my son a good quality of life. I took him to the top children's hospitals in the Delaware Valley. I did the research and asked the doctors all sorts of questions to get the best treatment possible. I tried to position him to get a heart transplant to help extend his life. I prayed and solicited prayers from across the country and had faith in God to provide everything he needed. I fought hard to keep my son here. I was given all kinds of accolades from our supporters of how strong I seemed to be. But on this last day in Marky's presence, I could see that he was tired. He had enough of this illness that incapacitated his body. Marky had already accepted Christ into his heart. He was ready to go. And at this point, I had to be strong enough to let him go.

CHALLENGE:

1. God can and will perform miracles in our lives today. What miracle are you looking for God to perform in your life?
2. What will you do or how will you respond if God doesn't perform the miracle that you want?
3. What are some scriptures you can find and tie them to the miracles you are believing God for?

PRAYER FOCUS: Loving Savior, thank You that You're always present in the storm. As I move through life's lowest moments, help me each day to recognize Your presence and the sometimes-hidden blessings that accompany every adversity I face.

April 12, 2007, 12:59 a.m.

He's Free...

Free from pain, free from sickness, free from worries. The Lord took Marky home to be with Him on Wednesday night April 11 at 7:36 p.m. He was ready and he went peacefully. To God be the glory! I will update you with more tomorrow. Thank you for your prayers and being with us on this extraordinary journey.

Love,
Dynita & Mark

Memories: I See Marky

A Poem by Rita Bristol
April 12, 2007

I see Marky on the ultrasound machine two months before his birth.

I see Marky being birthed into this world on May 23, 2000.

I see Marky fight the odds of abnormal birth. What was predicted to happen did not happen.

I see Marky jump up from a lying to a sitting position in bed. His eyes light up and a big smile come upon his face when he hears his mom's voice as she walks into his room a few days after his transfer from DuPont Hospital to Children's Hospital (This wonderful sight I will always hold dear to my heart.)

I see Marky's smiling face whenever his dad walks into his hospital room when he was at DuPont in the CICU. He'd be watching the clock for 6:00 p.m. when according to his mom, his dad was to come in the door. How his little face would light up.

I see Marky's smiling face when I walk into his room, a smile not as big as his smile for mom and dad, but still a smile nonetheless.

I see Marky smile even when he tried not to smile; all I had to say, "I see that smile coming through," he couldn't hold it back any longer; a little smile would peek through, then the big smile would follow.

I see Marky sitting in CHOP's activity room, making photo frames, cards for his mom, dad, sister, and grandparents.

I see Marky watching movies and playing games with his patient friend Ricky.

I see Marky make huge progress from not being able to walk at all, to being pushed in the wheelchair, to struggling on awkward legs to stand, to slowly riding a tricycle, to walking alone, to speeding up CHOP's cardiac unit, grinning, and almost running into some people.

I see Marky's smile when he and I talk about how nasty the hospital hamburgers taste.

I see Marky smiling as he sits outside of CHOP with his mom, Ricky, me, and their nurses. I see him laughing out loud as we spray him and Ricky with Spider-Man web spray, and they spray us back.

I see Marky on March 21 in the activity room at the "Mardi Gras" having his picture taken with me, making a frame for his picture, and his smile at seeing a clown walk on stilts.

I see Marky smile as he talks with some of his favorite people at CHOP—Moses, who kept his room clean, one of his favorite doctors Dr. Hannah, and many others.

I see Marky watching "Flushed Away" over and over, at least two to three times a day, then the same with "Monster House," "The Incredibles," and "Shrek."

I see Marky playing his games on the XBox.

I see Marky's face light up when Katelyn surprises him with a visit.

I see Marky smiling and laughing whenever Naomi was around. She kept him laughing.

I see Marky laughing out loud whenever he gave Naomi the play doctor's set, and she would jump on her mom's lap to hold her down so that he or she could give Dynita a needle. Oh, how he would get a big laugh out of that scene.

The last time I saw Marky smile was on April 3, around 7:30 p.m., when his dad stood in the doorway to surprise him with a visit. When Marky turned to see who was walking in the door, the biggest smile came on his face when he saw his dad. That was the day he was so weak and tired he could hardly stay awake. But through all that, his biggest smile that day was the sight of his dad.

I will see Marky's bright smile forever!

Thank you, God, for the angel You loaned to us for almost seven years.

Thank you, God, for the blessing you sent to us.

Thank you, God, that Marky is no longer suffering.

Thank you, God, that Marky is in heaven with You.

Now, Lord, please bless his mom, dad, and sister. Give them Your joy, peace, and understanding.

I See Marky!

Love Grandmom Rita

PART II

Recovering from Loss

CHAPTER 11

The New Normal

Blessed are those who mourn, for they will be comforted.
—Matthew 5:4 (NIV)

Shortly after we buried Marky, some close friends of ours blessed Mark and I with a weekend at their timeshare in Atlantic City. A one hour and fifteen minute drive took us away from it all; or so I thought. Unfortunately, the pain of our loss followed us. There was no running away from it, because it was engraved in our hearts. There had been so much time we spent apart from each other over the last four months. This was a good time for Mark and I to talk with each other and reconnect. We recommitted ourselves to support each other through this difficult time and declared we would not allow this tragedy to end our marriage. Whether on the mountain tops or in the valley lows, we were best friends, lovers, and partners for life.

After Mark and I checked into the resort, we visited the outlet stores to shop. Some people use retail therapy as a mechanism to cope with stress, but I was not in the mood. While inside the Nike store, Mark was trying to get me to pick out new sneakers. It was crowded, and all the people seemed to be in a hurry to buy up everything they could. But I just found a seat and sat down. I was not interested. Now my siblings knew that I could definitely use some new sneakers because I could easily still be wearing the royal blue and white LA Gears from my high school cheerleading days. I just had a philosophy that as long as they weren't worn out, I could still wear them. I was probably the person most in need of new sneakers in that store, but it really wasn't important to me. I didn't care. None of that mattered to me. All I kept thinking was, "I miss my son; I want to be where he is. God, come and get me now. Take me out of this misery." Mark finally convinced me to get some new sneakers, but they just didn't bring any joy to me as they did all the other consumers around me.

I later found a book store among the outlet stores. I went inside while Mark shopped at a nearby store. I needed solace. I needed answers. I needed hope to face tomorrow, to face reality when we returned home the next day. I found a section in the store on grieving. I perused several titles before coming across the books I would purchase. They all had something to offer me to get me through my time of bereavement. I read, and read, and read over the next few weeks. This helped to build up hope for a brighter future.

Somehow, Mark and I picked up the pieces and dragged ourselves out of bed every day to move forward. We went to grief counseling at our church for a few weeks. I highly recommend counseling for any family who has suffered a loss. I went to the cemetery almost every day for the first month or two. I was so used to taking care of Marky every day that I wanted to be near him. I had dreams about Marky all the time, daydreams and night dreams. I dreamed he would walk through my bedroom door to say good morning and turn on the TV to watch his morning cartoons. Then I woke up and realized that would never happen again.

After two weeks, Mark returned to work at Princeton University. Personally, I thought it was too soon for him. But he felt the need to get back to something normal and take his mind off the sadness that lingered. His job was really supportive and understanding. Mark wanted to know when I planned to return to substitute teaching. I was in no rush. I was not ready, and I wasn't going to let him or anybody else rush me back to work. I had Naomi back in school. And I was still writing thank you cards and reading books to help ease my pain and build my strength.

I have to admit something that may sound terrible as a Christian. I was disappointed with God's decision to take Marky home. I accepted Jesus Christ as my Savior at eight years old. I read and studied the Bible for many years and had come to believe what it said. I knew many of the scriptures on healing. I had been reciting them, professing them, and standing on them ever since Marky's first pre-diagnosis. We had believed God for a new heart for Marky. I saw several kids in the hospital go through the process of the heart transplant, and I believed with all my heart that God wanted that for Marky too. I imagined him healthy again. I envisioned him in the backyard playing catch with a football. I stayed positive and prayed the scriptures over Marky daily. But after everything was said and done, the answer to my prayer seemed to be a hard *No*. I didn't believe the scriptures were for me. I felt like they were for everyone else, but God had overlooked my prayers. I didn't understand why He took Marky away. I was doing fine taking care of him. I gave him his meds on time, took him to his medical appointments, made sure he went to his therapy sessions and everything. I was serving God faithfully with the gifts He gave me. I paid my tithes and gave offerings. But all that still wasn't enough to move the hand of God to heal Marky on earth. This was disheartening for me. Please don't get me wrong. I wasn't angry with God, and I continued to serve him. I did my best to be encouraging to others around me who were going through their own crises. But I felt overlooked, plain and simple, overlooked.

I remember having a conversation with Aunt Pleasant after the burial. I needed to talk to her because she had firsthand experience of losing a son. She had identical twin boys, Ronald and Donald. And when they were ten years old, Donald drowned in the Delaware River. It was a horrible tragedy that brought sadness to my family and the entire town. So there I was talking to a woman who had lost a child through tragedy. Surely she had a word for me.

I sought her wisdom. I asked her, "Will my heart ever heal? Will this pain ever go away? I just can't imagine going through the rest of my life with this agonizing pain."

She smiled and said, "Yes, dear; yes, your heart will heal. You will always feel the loss in your heart, but each day that goes by, your heart will hurt a little less."

She gave me a big hug. I wanted to believe her so much. I wanted to feel relief from this pain. It seemed almost unbearable. But I have to say, she was right. My heart feels so much better now, fourteen years later. Time has definitely been a contributing factor to the healing process.

Some people are of the school of thought that time heals. I learned that it is not necessarily time that heals you, but what you do during the time that brings about the healing. If I didn't go to counseling, if I didn't continue to read God's Word and surround myself with other believers who encouraged me, if I didn't read books on grieving and start integrating myself back into normal life activities, I don't think I would have experienced healing as I eventually did. So in that sense, yes, time does heal.

We Saw Heaven

I remember the visitation week leading up to my son's homegoing service. The house was packed with people. Our friends and family had come to see about us and give their sincere condolences. It is common for folks to bring comfort food, baked goods, flowers, and cards. However, I distinctly remember a friend of ours from church gave us the book *We Saw Heaven* by Roberts Liardon. I thanked him for his thoughtfulness. At that very moment, I could not read it because there was so much going on around me. It felt like I was in a whirlwind, my body was exhausted, and I needed to focus on preparing for the funeral service. So I graciously accepted the book and took it up to my bedroom. As I did with many books, I placed it on top of a short stack of books next to my nightstand. I was in the process of reading or planned to read them shortly.

After all the crowds of people diminished, the house was quiet again. We were all searching for something. Searching for the answers to the questions: Why did you take our Marky, Lord? Why didn't you heal him on earth so we could see him grow up to live a long life? We knew you were able to heal him. You are Jehovah Rophe, the healer. Weren't we taking good care of him? What is Marky doing in heaven now? Is he sleeping peacefully? Is he running around carefree in heaven with his dog Yoey? Is he periodically looking down over us, checking to see what we're doing? Is he missing us as much as we are missing him? Aren't we good Christian people? We went to church regularly, paid our tithes and gave offerings. We served in several ministries at our church. We were kind to our neighbors. We prayed and prayed and fasted and prayed some more. We quoted the scriptures of healing and declared good health and wholeness over Marky. I even called a TV evangelist's prayer line and gave a monetary donation in exchange for a prayer for a miracle to save my son's life. My last-ditch effort to bring back my son in the waning hours, where I could sense him slipping away, had failed (in my opinion).

Yes, I had lots of questions for God. As a mother and the primary caretaker of our two children, it was top priority for me to know where my kids were at all times and what they were doing. So with the house quieted now, I had time to crack open this new book. In the book, *We Saw Heaven*, the author wrote about several accounts of those who had gone to heaven and returned with vivid pictures and scenarios of what heaven looks like. I was glued to the pages because I wanted to know what it was like in the new realm my son had recently entered. In many regards, the accounts gave me peace of mind. There are descriptions of beautiful flowers and trees, the most delicious fruit one would ever taste, and the refreshingly cool bodies of water made me yearn to experience that kind of peace. I didn't want to put the book down but would fall asleep with the book in my bed. On the other hand, other chapters in the book confused me, and one even angered me.

Liardon describes the account of an eight-year-old boy experiencing heaven. The boy saw three storehouses filled with lots of different body parts on the shelves—body parts of different sizes and colors to reflect the diverse population on earth. God told the boy these were the body parts for people on earth who needed them. They were the unclaimed blessings. But some people didn't get them because they didn't pray and believe God would provide them. I was upset with God because we prayed. My family prayed. My church family prayed. Various prayer groups were praying. People I didn't even know, who had somehow heard about Marky's illness, were praying for his healing. We were bombarding heaven with our prayers—banging on the doors of heaven for God to send him a new heart or to repair the heart he had from birth. We pleaded. My grandmother Sylvia, who is a prayer warrior, even told me that she tried to bargain with God and asked him to take her instead of Marky. And yet Marky's life was not spared. This just didn't set right with me. I knew the Scriptures and I believed God's Word by faith. What about these scriptures?

Therefore I tell you, whatever you ask in prayer,
believe that you have received it, and it will be yours.
—Mark 11:24 (ESV)

~

He sent His word and healed them,
and delivered them from their destructions.
—Psalm 107:20 (NKJV)

~

If you abide in Me, and My words abide in you,
you will ask what you desire, and it shall be done for you.
—John 15:7 (NKJV)

I had seen God heal others before. God healed my cousin, Terrence, of a heart murmur when he was a baby. When we would go swimming together as children, I was reminded of his healing because we could see the scar that ran down his chest. He is still alive today after over forty years.

God performed a miracle for my husband's oldest brother Michael (Mike) when he was age nineteen. In 1983, while in his second year of college, Mike was in a terrible car accident. He was rushed to the hospital with severe swelling on the brain, which led him into a coma. The doctor did not expect him to live and told his mother if he lived, he would be a vegetable. Mom Rita and her sister Kathleen would visit Mike every day in the hospital and talked positively in his ears, trying to wake him up. On the third day of the coma, Mike finally cracked his eyes open and turned his head to look at her. The nurses were crying with joy, and the doctor was amazed at what they witnessed. They nicknamed him the miracle boy. After three months of much prayer, faith, medical attention, and rehabilitation,

Michael learned to talk, walk, and regain his short-term memory again. Many years later, Mike graduated from the Wharton School of Business and became a successful salesman. This family knew the power of prayer and what having faith in God could do.

I believed God's Word was true, but those scriptures of healing didn't apply to me. They pertained to other people but just not to me. It was a very hard pill to swallow. I struggled with this for months.

A few weeks after Marky's funeral, my husband and I went to grief counseling at our church. This helped us to understand and recognize the stages of grief. The common reactions people have as they try to make sense of a loss are 1) denial, numbness, and shock; 2) bargaining; 3) depression; 4) anger; 5) acceptance. We wanted to work our way through these stages together. However, I realized that we were experiencing them at different levels and at different times. I had to give my husband the space he needed to grieve at his own pace and in his own way. At times there was contention in our home because we were processing our loss and grieving at different stages. However, over time, we learned how to support each other through the varying phases of grief.

I gradually integrated myself back into life. It felt like I hadn't been in a grocery store in a few weeks, so I was feeling a little out of sorts as I went down the aisles to shop for food. Everywhere I turned, there was a reminder that my son wasn't here anymore. I no longer needed to buy the bottles of red Gatorade for him to mix in the MiraLAX. I no longer needed to buy plums or the snack-size pepperoni slices because he was the only one who ate those foods in my house. I found myself on the verge of tears because I missed buying the foods he liked.

I went back to substitute teaching about five weeks after we buried my son. I would usually make myself available to work at any school in the county, but this time I only signed up to work at

Marky's elementary school. I knew the principals, many of the teachers, and best of all, I knew the students who were Marky's classmates and friends. Some people may think it was strange that I would go back to his school with all the reminders that he was no longer there, but I felt a sense of comfort when I was with the school community because it was warm, friendly, and consoling. I think having me there helped them heal as well.

Gradually, I integrated myself back into the mainstream of life. It felt like I was coming out of my bubble. We enjoyed an overnight Elisha Family Reunion in Baltimore, Maryland, in July. My family continued to shower us with love and support. We even designated a day when everyone wore their Marky t-shirt. I rejoined the Worship choir and Women's Ensemble at my church and started attending Mocha Moms events again. Bit by bit, I was putting the pieces of my life back together.

Delayed Grief

My daughter Mimi was always fun-loving and playful like most four-year-olds. She enjoyed making other people laugh. When Marky was in the hospital, she would do her best to try to cheer him up. But now her playmate was gone. It took some time for her to process that he really wasn't coming back. It was confusing to hear us say Marky died, but we would one day see him again. She recalled the night of his funeral when the visitors passed by our front row seats of the church to give their condolences. When the casket closed, and then we buried the casket in the ground the next morning, it finally clicked for her. She understood that he had really gone away. Marky went to heaven to be with God, and she would not see him anymore until she goes to heaven too.

The first Monday after Marky's burial was difficult. Mimi probably thought it was strange that I didn't wake her up for school that morning. She woke up on her own and came into my bedroom to find me sitting at the foot of the bed staring at the floor. I was lost in my thoughts. She jumped onto my lap and hugged me for a long time. We both began to cry and console one another, wishing Marky could be with us or that we could be with him. The pain was so great that I secretly wanted God to take the three of us to be with him so we could all be together again. However, I knew that was not his will. We'd have to walk out this excruciating journey of grief. Even though I had overslept that morning, I thought it was important to get back to somewhat of a normal schedule. Mimi said she wanted to go to school, so I got us ready for the day and took her back to Abundant Life Preparatory School (ALPS).

After establishing a new routine for Mimi, she seemed to go back to her normal, energetic self. I watched her closely for any signs of grief. Loneliness was the most prevalent. To counter the loneliness, she spent a lot of time with her cousins and friends. Our friends with kids were so supportive and would volunteer to pick up Mimi so she would have playtime with kids her age. Every weekend, either kids were at our house or she was at their house spending time. This certainly helped to fill the void.

We thought it would also be helpful to give Mimi's bedroom a makeover. My sister helped me transform what previously had been the kids' bedroom into Mimi's bedroom. We removed Marky's blue race car bed and pulled down the Spider-Man posters from the wall. The walls were painted lavender and pink, with a splash of yellow. Three cube size shelves with heart-shaped cutouts hung above her princess castle bed, which held her collection of crowns. It had truly become a princess' bedroom.

It wasn't until Mimi was about eight years old that she experienced an onset of grief. On the car ride home from a visit at a relative's house, she broke down in tears in the back seat of the car.

I was in the front seat driving and couldn't see her, but I turned down the radio so I could hear her. She asked, "Was it my fault that Marky collapsed and died?" I was stunned to hear this question, which seemed to come out of nowhere. She explained that while she was in the backyard playing with her relatives, Marky's name came up in the conversation. Mimi was saying he is gone now, but she was okay about it.

Then someone said, "Well, Marky had heart disease, and y'all were playing tag, right, when he was about to die?"

This took Mimi by surprise. "What?" She said, "No, we were just playing. I don't think that's what happened."

The person pushed a little more and said, "Well, I mean, he collapsed and then he was in the hospital for a really long time."

From that conversation, Mimi thought the whole incident was her fault and she felt responsible for his death. After all these years had passed, it suddenly occurred to her that it was possibly her fault that her brother died. She went into a long period of depression and blamed herself for his death. She thought, "If I hadn't been playing with him like that... Maybe I shouldn't have been playing with him like that." I tried to console her and let her know that there was nothing wrong with them playing together.

By this time, we were in her bedroom and I was putting her to bed. Mimi continued to ask me, "Mom, was it my fault? Was it my fault?" as she was sobbing with her face in her hands. I sat on the side of her twin bed and tried to console her and explain over and over again that it wasn't her fault. Marky had a weak heart, and it was going to happen at some point. It just happened to be while they were playing, but it wasn't because they were playing. This conversation led her into a deep sadness. She began to have dreams about Marky when he was alive and would replay the scene of the night he collapsed. I arranged one-on-one counseling for Mimi right away to help her deal with this grief. Over time with the therapist, she was able to talk about what she was feeling and gain a better understanding. Counseling proved to be helpful for her, and she could move forward without guilt or blame.

Over the years, I watched how Mimi interacted with her friends. Her close friends knew that her brother was deceased. Some of their older siblings happen to be Marky's classmates, so they were already aware. Many of them participated in the annual Have a Heart Day fundraiser and essay contest held at the school in memory of Marky. Mimi also found lots of social support through the various soccer teams she played on. She had several friends and was often the life of the party. Mimi admitted that while growing up without a sibling, she was envious of those who had siblings. She missed having a brother terribly. She would caution her friends not to wish they didn't have a sibling. From her perspective, even if your sibling gets on your nerves, at least you have them. She acknowledged that she felt more comfortable when she was playing with other kids who didn't have any siblings. She felt like they could understand her situation better.

After we relocated to West Virginia at the end of Mimi's seventh-grade year, I noticed a difference. Not only did she prefer to be called Naomi instead of her childhood nickname Mimi, but Naomi did not outright tell her new friends and classmates that her older brother was deceased. None of them knew our backstory, and she preferred it that way. When her friends would visit our home and saw the family photos on the wall, that sparked the conversation about Marky and I could tell Naomi was uncomfortable talking about him. She would quickly breeze over it in casual conversation, "Oh yeah, that's my older brother Marky. He died a long time ago." And then she would hastily change the subject and move the conversation along to another topic. She felt like it was not just awkward for her, but it was awkward for her friends because they often didn't know what to say.

I even noticed Naomi continued this pattern when we moved to Maryland in her sophomore year of high school. In a recent conversation with her, she revealed that very few of her high school friends and none of her college friends know about her brother Marky. She preferred to keep that part of her life to herself unless the person enters her inner circle. She admitted that she doesn't want to be overcome by her emotions or sadness while she's at school or around her friends.

I definitely noticed the transition from younger Mimi to older Naomi. Now that she's older, she posts on social media about Marky's birthday and the anniversary of his death, which I think are steps in the right direction. I shared with her that continued therapy could be helpful to move her further along on the journey to healing. It is a long journey, and everyone must go at their own pace.

Challenge:

1. Grief is a feeling of loss when one loses a close family member, friend, a job, income, pet, or when a major change in life occurs, such as divorce, moving, kids leaving home, and even retiring. What loss are you grieving today? What are you doing to process your grief?

2. How have you walked through the stages of grief?

3. Be sure to give yourself ample time to experience your thoughts and feelings. Talk to a trusted friend about the loss. Express your feelings openly or write in your journal about it. It is okay to cry and release the feelings.

4. If you feel stuck and need help processing your grief, seek professional counseling to help you work through

the stages of grief. Contact your Human Resources department at work. Many employers provide counseling resources for their staff for free or little charge. Attend group therapy sessions which are often offered at churches, hospitals, and community agencies.

PRAYER FOCUS: Dear God, thank You for Your comforting presence in my pain and sorrow. Help me in turn to be a comfort to others.

CHAPTER 12

Double For My Trouble

Because you got a double dose of trouble and more than your share of contempt, Your inheritance in the land will be doubled and your joy go on forever.
—Isaiah 61:7 (The Message)

In 2010, Naomi was now an only child at eight years old, and we could tell she really missed having her brother. In turn, we missed having another child in the house with us. When Marky died, it left a huge void in our lives. We missed him terribly and tried all sorts of approaches to move forward.

I can recall the time when my husband was very upset with me because I had decided to get my fallopian tubes tied shortly after Naomi was born in 2002. Although Marky had the heart condition, I never actually thought Naomi would one day be an only child. I just never thought the disease would take him out like it did. I had faith in God that Marky's body would be healed and we would see him grow up and have children of his own. So a year or so after he passed away, I noticed that my husband started questioning if I could possibly have another baby. And I said, "Noooooo, that boat had sailed." I realized how insensitive that comment was to a father who had lost his only son, his namesake, and he wanted another chance to father more children.

I could tell it was really bothering him, so the next time I went to my OB-GYN physician, I asked if the tubal ligation could be reversed. The doctor informed me that the process he used involved burning the ends of the tubes so they would be permanently closed. There was no way to reverse the procedure. I was a little disappointed by this news. I questioned myself, "Should I have waited longer before deciding to get my tubes tied? Did I act prematurely?" This burdened my heart. The only thing I could do at this point was pray that God would open up another avenue for us to expand our family.

One Sunday after church, we met a married couple who were new to our congregation. I was complimenting their beautiful baby girl, who was cozy in her stroller. As I got to know the couple, I learned they had adopted all three of their kids….as babies—two boys and a girl. I was amazed at how God had molded them into a beautiful vibrant family. I could see their kids were thriving because they were in a loving home and being nurtured. We began to spend time with them and get to know their story more. My girlfriend encouraged us to research the process of going through the Department of Youth and Family Services (DYFS) to become foster parents. We began looking into the process. This could be just what our family needed.

We missed having another child in our family. We knew Mimi was very lonely, and she was pretty vocal about wanting me to have another baby. Mark and I prayed about it and discussed it at length until we finally decided to move forward with the plan to get certified to become foster parents. A social worker came out to our home to explain the process and got us started with the paperwork. There was a lot of paperwork with about 1,000 questions. Our friends walked alongside us through the long and taxing process. We read the materials and attended many online webinars and in-person classes and events. After completing a certain number of hours of training and passing the background checks, we were finally certified to become foster parents with the intent to adopt.

On a Wednesday evening in mid-December 2010, I was sitting in a booth at Amato's Pizza restaurant with my Granddaddy. We had just come from his dialysis session which was right down the street. While waiting for our pizza to be baked, we were just talking and shooting the breeze. Suddenly, I felt a buzz on my right leg. The cell phone in my coat pocket was buzzing to notify me that a voicemail message was sent. I decided to check my messages while we waited. Our social worker called to say they had two little boys who were brothers and needed housing immediately. They were in temporary housing, but they were available for us to meet and to consider for foster care. I told my granddaddy about the call and explained we needed to take our pizza to go. I hurried home to give Mark the news. Mark was excited to hear there were two African American boys, ages one and three, who needed a home and a family. This was not the first phone call I received from the social worker about an available child. We had turned down several others because we did not feel it was the right fit. However, this seemed different. We were excited about this opportunity. So we prayed together first, and I called the social worker back to express our interest in meeting the boys.

The boys arrived at our house on Friday evening. The emergency foster mom who brought them described them as good little boys who needed some tender loving care. Since they were afraid of her dogs, she wouldn't be able to keep them. She gave us a quick rundown of the foods they liked to eat, medications, and the clothes in the overnight bag. They were only coming for a twenty-four-hour trial visit. Naomi was smiling from ear to ear as she welcomed them to our home and showed them where some of the toys were. I was busy jotting down notes of everything the woman was telling me, hoping I would remember the key things she said. I wanted this to be the perfect overnight visit.

The evening with the boys started out fine. We had a few family members stop by the house to meet them. The boys were smiling and seemed happy to be here. I would imagine it was a little overwhelming for them, meeting some strangers in this unfamiliar house. What do you do when you want to welcome guests and make them feel comfortable? You feed them. So I cooked some dinner so we could sit down at the table together to eat and get to know each other. They didn't hold back on expressing themselves. The youngest one ate so much food that he vomited twice. And the oldest one got so angry with his little brother while playing with the toys in the family room that he bit him on the arm, leaving teeth marks. We ran to quickly separate them and give them a good talking to about how to play nicely with one another. Even though it was a rough night, we were glad we got to see the boys in their rawest form.

Since both sets of clothes for the little one were spoiled, I put a load of laundry in the washing machine, so he would have clean clothes for the next day. Later on, we got them ready for bed. One of them needed a nebulizer treatment for the asthma. "Oh, I could handle this," I thought to myself. I was used to giving those treatments to Naomi, who also had asthma. They enjoyed Naomi reading them a bedtime story while they were tucked under the covers wearing their cute pajamas.

This bedroom previously doubled as the guestroom and my home office. My extra clothes that didn't fit into my walk-in closet were also stored in there. However, part of the agreement with fostering kids is, they needed to have their own room. So about eleven months prior, Mark and I decided to move my office into Mark's home office, as long as I could keep my side of the room neat. It was not the ideal situation for either of us because we both liked having our own space. I mean, we already shared a bedroom and the rest of the house together. But this was the sacrifice we were willing to make so we could open up our home and expand our family.

It was not an easy task getting the boys to sleep. They were highly energetic and easily excited at the least little thing. Besides, they were in a new place with new people. We were probably seeing some nervous energy. But little did they know, we were nervous too and were trying to put our best foot forward. After a while, we got them to doze off to sleep as the lullaby music played on the CD in the background. This was one of my secret weapons for putting Naomi and Marky to sleep when they were little.

At the end of the night, Mark and I sat down together, looked at each other, and took a deep breath. Were we really ready to take on this challenge of becoming foster parents? Were we ready to dedicate the next possible twenty years of our lives raising these kids? Yes, we were. Despite the bumpy ride we encountered that night, we felt like we could make a difference in their lives. So why not? Let's take the plunge.

We made the final decision to bring them into our home on a more permanent basis. They arrived only days before Christmas. The extended family was so excited for us. Our house hadn't been filled with so much noise and excitement on Christmas morning in six years. It looked chaotic with boxes, bags, torn wrapping paper, toys, and clothes everywhere. It sounded like a crazy house too, with high pitch shrieks and shouts of joy because they received some new shiny toys. Nonetheless, in a strange way, it was music to our ears. It was the fulfillment of a prayer request and lots of preparation. We knew God would provide everything we needed to take care of our family of five.

During their stay with us, Naomi felt a sense of purpose because she took pride in helping out with the boys. She played with them and helped set up evening activities for them while I was cooking or grading school papers. She looked after them when they played outside in the yard. Naomi enjoyed being an older sister and having some extra responsibilities around the house.

We took the boys everywhere. It was very important to us to build a foundation of God in their lives. They went to our church and made friends in the toddler room class. We took them to Naomi's soccer games, the movies, the Camden Riversharks baseball games, swimming lessons at the YMCA, the playgrounds, the zoo, and roller skating. On a hot summer day, we took a day trip with some close friends and family to NYC to see the Statue of Liberty and visited the largest Toys "R" Us store in the country. We were super excited to ride the giant indoor Ferris wheel and take pictures with Iron Man and Spider-Man. We had a ball with our newfound sons. I don't know who had more fun, the adults or the kids. Sometimes, Naomi would tease them and get a big kick out of scaring her brothers with the rubber spiders and lizards she would get from the local dollar store. They disliked when she did that. We taught them the alphabet and how to spell their names. We took time to read with them every day to build their sense of adventure and imagination and to hopefully instill a love for reading.

On the other hand, it wasn't all fun and games. We had to do a fair amount of disciplining them as well. No doubt, these kids had been through a lot. They were confused, scared, and sometimes angry. We taught them how to get along with each other and when they interacted with other kids. Sometimes Naomi and the boys even argued and disagreed about stuff. Nevertheless, we loved on them even more to let them know we were here to stay as long as they needed us. We went through what normal families went through. We were just grateful to experience wholeness again.

Mark and I had high hopes to eventually adopt the boys and make them permanent members of our family. We loved them and they clearly loved us. However, weekly visitations with their biological parents started up again. The social worker said this was standard procedure, but we could probably still adopt them. The primary goal of DYFS, after safety, is reunification with the biological family. The more they visited their birth family, the more they were torn between the two families. Although I knew they enjoyed living with us, they loved their mother, father, and siblings very much, and they preferred to live with them. Most kids want to be with their birth parents; that is a common perspective. I could not fault them for feeling this way.

At that time, the New Jersey law was for the kids and youth to either be reunified with their biological parents or the parents' rights would be terminated by the fifteenth month. Their case was presented in court, and the judge ruled for the boys to be reunited with their mother and father. That was that. We had no say in the matter. The final decision was made, so once again, our hearts were broken. We had to come to grips that we couldn't adopt them as planned. It was out of our hands.

Our foster sons stayed with us for a total of fourteen months. We had approximately three weeks to prepare them and ourselves for their departure. I prayed and asked God what I could do in the time we had left to ease the transition. He impressed on my heart to get them dedicated to the Lord through our church. I expressed this desire with my pastors, and they agreed to support us. My brother-in-law, Reverend Darryl, performed the dedication service right in our home. I dressed the boys alike in black pants, a black shirt, and a dark red vest. No shoes were needed since we were in our home. I put together some appetizers and dessert and invited our immediate family members over to witness this occasion and give their blessing as well.

Some may be wondering what the significance of a baby or child dedication is. It is not equivalent to a child giving their life to Christ and receiving salvation because usually, a dedication is done before they are at the age to make such a decision. Traditional baby dedications involve a charge to the parents and chosen godparents to raise the child in a Christian home, expose them to Christian values and beliefs and demonstrate godly character before the child. The goal is for the child to eventually make their own decision to follow Christ. However, in this case, there were no godparents to appoint. And in a short time, they would not be under our direct care. We simply wanted to cover our sons with the blessing of the Lord wherever their journey would take them in life.

This excerpt from Rev. Darryl Washington's eulogy at Marky's celebration of life service clearly explains the purpose of a baby dedication.

"Why do we perform baby dedications in the church?

—Because we want to present them to the Lord, and for our Pastors & leaders to convey a blessing over their lives.

—So that as they grow in stature and in the knowledge of the Lord, they may discover their divine purpose, and pursue it with all diligence.

—That they may subject their entire person to the Lordship of Jesus Christ, and the governance of God.

—And that when their journey (on earth) is over,
they would leave a permanent mark on their generation,
and be an enduring witness for others.

Mark and Dynita knew this was the best thing they
could ever do for their children."

Darryl was absolutely right. The best thing we as parents could do for any of our children was to teach them to love God and be loved by God. To teach them they had a Heavenly Father who created them and cared about them. I wanted them to know that no matter how bad they felt or what trouble they faced, God was with them and would make it alright for them.

Our foster sons left our home in February of 2012. The answer to our prayers was now walking out the front door. We were sad and disappointed about this drastic change in our lives. How would we move on from another traumatic loss? It was not nearly the same level of grief as when Marky died because these boys would still be alive and in good health. Nonetheless, we felt a void. We felt an emptiness when they departed. Maybe I set myself up for this failure. After all, foster care is designed to be temporary custody with the goal to reunify the family. Somehow I felt caught off guard. I was expecting it to be a pathway to adoption similar to my girlfriend's experience with her three kids. However, I was now faced with another season of grief.

I recently found an article online called "9 Things Foster Parents Want You to Know About the Foster Care System."[4] There are many rewards of being a foster parent. Being there to support foster children during the toughest times of their lives makes a big difference. However, the writer warns there are highs and lows that every foster parent should know before starting. He interviewed several foster care parents and found these are the top nine things you should know when considering fostering.

1. Foster care is temporary. It is not a permanent solution.
2. Love them as if they were your own children. Don't hold back. Love on them hard.

3. Be patient with the kids. They are scared and confused.
4. Be patient with the caseworkers. They are often overworked and unpaid.
5. Be patient with their birth parents as they work on themselves to become better parents.
6. Be patient with yourself. It is a hard job. Take care of yourself. Remember why you said yes in the first place.
7. Be prepared for questions. Remind family members not to ask awkward questions in front of the kids.
8. Be prepared to let go. You will probably get hurt and experience grief.
9. Find a support system. There are many resources available to guide you through the many aspects of fostering.

Thankfully our story with the boys didn't end there. It turns out that we are still in touch with our foster sons to this present day. After they left our home, I prayed and asked God to help us to stay in contact with them. Although they didn't become our permanent sons, God gave us the opportunity to continue loving on them and being a part of their lives as they grow up. We established a relationship with their birth parents, and they agreed to let us see the boys periodically. They would come to stay the weekends with us, and we took them to church and other family events. They even traveled to West Virginia when we relocated there in the summer of 2015. We have spent a couple of Christmas breaks together in our home in Maryland and even took them on a vacation to Orlando, Florida. Now that they are adolescents, they reach out to us through social media and through their cell phones. I keep in touch with their grandpop, who now has full custody of them. It's a truly unique relationship that not everyone experiences. But I believe God custom made what we needed in order to heal from the separation and move forward. The way I see it is that He delivered a double blessing to us for our trouble.

What was most profound to me about this relationship is that it was the source of redemption for both parties. These two little boys needed us to care for them and protect them while they were in their most vulnerable state. Their home life was disrupted, and they temporarily lost their birth parents. They, too, were in a state of grief and loss. At the same time, my family needed the boys just as much while we were still in mourning, seeking restoration from our loss of Marky. Our time together led us down a path toward healing and wholeness.

I remember part of our bedtime routine when I tucked the boys into their bunked beds at night, after they brushed their teeth and used the bathroom. I would pray for the boys, and then they each took a turn to offer up a short prayer to God, which almost always included prayers for their birth parents and their grandpop. We would quiet ourselves and reflect on what we did that day. The boys would recount their favorite parts of the day. And we would say out loud, "It was a good day." As I reflect on those particularly precious fourteen months we had them in our care, I can also say, "It was a good day."

CHALLENGE:

1. What are you willing to sacrifice to make room for the blessing you've been waiting for?
2. How has God helped you to heal from your loss?
3. What additional steps do you need to take to experience healing or to move closer to your healing?

PRAYER FOCUS: Heavenly Father, thank You for loving me so much that You would turn my pain into purpose. Thank You for giving me the ability to help others as You are healing me.

CHAPTER 13

4 Steps to L.I.V.E. Again

God comforts us in all our troubles, so that we can comfort those in any trouble with the comfort we ourselves receive from God.
—2 Corinthians 1:4 (NIV)

President Joe Biden once said, "Losing a son, daughter, brother, sister, mom, or dad is like losing a piece of your soul." This is coming from one who knows the pain of grief all too well. Shortly after Joe Biden was initially elected to be a U.S. senator, he lost his first wife and daughter in a tragic car accident in 1972, and much later in life in 2015, he bore the death of his beloved son. Mr. Biden was sworn into the office of the Senate while in a Delaware hospital while his two sons were being treated for serious injuries sustained in the accident that took their mother and baby sister. I wonder how he did it. How did he find the strength to keep moving forward while being devastated with such a tremendous loss at a pivotal time in his career?

I had to figure this out for myself. How would I move forward in my life after losing my dear son? As much as I wanted to crawl up in a ball and die, deep inside, I knew I had so much more to live for. My dear husband and daughter loved and needed me. We needed each other to get through this time of grief and sorrow. As I look back over my life, and the events that took place, I can see how I was able to move forward. I learned how to love my family and friends, and I looked for opportunities to find the bright side and laugh. I found my village and leaned into them on the journey through grief. I had to evaluate my well-being and administer self-care to regain strength and a sober mind. I took the opportunity to encourage others along the way, either in their grief or getting through some other tough times in their lives.

The Lord gave me the acronym L.I.V.E. as the four steps to move forward after losing my child. It stands for **L**ove hard and laugh often, **I**nclude others on the journey, check your **V**ital signs, and **E**ncourage somebody else.

L— Love Hard and Laugh Often

Each day that we wake up and open our eyes is a new opportunity to love and be loved. Whether we see the sun shining or hear the raindrops pounce on the window, it is another chance to live and fulfill our purpose. Those who are reading this book now have lived through the coronavirus pandemic of 2020–2021. At the time of this writing, COVID-19 has claimed the lives of nearly 600,000 Americans and about 3.7 million globally. We are living through extremely sad times when people of every age, race, and gender are dying prematurely, leaving behind a multitude of grieving souls. Now more than ever, we need to adopt an attitude of gratitude because we are still here.

Why are we still here? To love. We are still here to experience the ultimate love of God and to show love, not only to our family and friends but to our neighbors, coworkers, acquaintances, and even strangers. Remember the popular song by Dionne Warwick? "What the world needs now is love, sweet love. It's the only thing that there's just too little of." Don't be afraid to love hard, which means loving with your whole heart, mind, and resources. I used to think the cliché love hurts was true. But after reading this quote by Meša Selimović, I have a different perspective.

Everyone says love hurts, but that is not true. Loneliness hurts.
Rejection hurts. Losing someone hurts. Envy hurts.
Everyone gets these things confused with love, but in reality,
love is the only thing in this world that covers up all pain
and makes someone feel wonderful again.
Love is the only thing in this world that does not hurt.

I loved hard when I was willing to sacrifice my own comfort in order to bring two little boys into our home. I loved hard when I was determined to continue our relationship with them even after they left our home. I loved hard when I organized the fundraiser to support sick children and their families, most of whom I would never meet. In the midst of showing love to others in need, my grieving heart was being mended.

Laughter is another way we experience healing in our mind, heart, and soul. Here is a journal entry I wrote while Marky was in the hospital. Let me take you back to a day when I saw the power of laughter at work.

Laughter Is Good Medicine for the Soul

It had been another grueling day for Marky. He woke up to yet another encounter with the phlebotomist. Marky's fears start rising and the tears begin to flow. Oh, how this six-year-old boy longed to just wake up to the sound of his little sister calling his name or to soft music that his mommy usually played in the mornings. But for now, it was the perpetual dread of the hospital blues. Taking medicines, getting needles, frequent examinations, invasion of privacy, and the constant beeping sounds of the medicine pump alarms, which had become the background noise for the past three months.

Once again, he only took a small bite of the fresh watermelon he requested and ignored the fried egg white and bacon with no fat, prepared especially the way he liked it. He told the nurse and me that he wasn't hungry yet but would eat it later. Mmhmm, right Marky. We knew what that meant. That meal will really be unappealing to him when he returned from his morning school and physical therapy sessions. He was glad at least to get out of his room.

Each person he encountered throughout the day tried to get Marky in a good mood. But he only managed a few smirks and, at best, a chuckle before remembering the sad reality. He was stuck in this hospital until a new heart arrived for him.

By the end of the day, he had had enough of all the medical staff prodding him, and he was even tired of his mom's continual pleas for him to eat. Then he heard a familiar voice say, "Hey Mark!" He looked up and surprisingly saw his best friend Katelyn and her mom. A huge grin lined his face. Immediately his demeanor changed as he began to play with his buddy from school. He got down on the floor mat with her, and they partnered to put a puzzle together and played a few games. They laughed and joked and acted silly like normal six-year-olds. He forgot about his worries, his discomforts, and what loomed in his uncertain future. It didn't matter. He was a kid again. I just sat back and enjoyed the essence of my son doing his best to live, laugh, and love despite the life-threatening trials he faced. For three hours, he laughed and played and was completely healed in his mind.

Proverbs 17:22 says, "A merry heart does good, like medicine, but a broken spirit dries the bones." And Proverbs 15:15 says, "All the days of the afflicted are evil, but he who is of a merry heart has a continual feast." A God-given cheerful heart can brighten even the days of the afflicted. That short time spent with Marky's best friend, Katelyn, recharged his battery and gave him the strength to get through the tough days ahead. It's amazing what laughter can do.

I— Include Others on the Journey

Shortly after Marky's funeral, my Uncle Eric proposed the idea to have a t-shirt created to memorialize Marky. We decided on the last school photo of Marky encased by a red heart with the caption, "The Boy With a Big Heart." At first, I was thinking this would be nice to distribute just to the family members. However, so many people in the community wanted to help that we decided to include the B. Bernice Young Elementary School (BYS). I partnered with Marky's first-grade teacher, Ms. Leibowitz, and she helped to get the fundraiser approved by the Board of Education. With the support of the school principal, Dr. King, Have a Heart Day was born.

Ms. Leibowitz introduced the idea of having a tree planted in Marky's memory on the school playground. It was one of his favorite places to be where he would run free, laugh, smile, and play with his friends. On the playground was where he could just be a kid. The BYS Family Association also had another tree planted and a bench dedicated in Marky's memory in the school's courtyard.

While Ms. Leibowitz's class was wrapping up their science series about butterflies, she had the clever idea for her class to release the butterflies in a short outdoor ceremony right next to Marky's tree. We all wore the Marky t-shirts or a red shirt because that was Marky's favorite color. A poem called "He Showed Us With His Smile" was written and read aloud by his first-grade teacher. Ms. Nanni and Mr. Snell brought their kindergarten class outside for the ceremony as well. I placed a huge red bow on the tree. It was a good opportunity for the students to have a dedicated time to remember their friend and classmate. I would imagine it was a source of healing for the students and the teachers, especially those who knew and worked closely with Marky.

This turned into an annual event and fundraiser that occurred during the week of Marky's birthday for the next seven years. Each year the merchandise grew, including heart-shaped soft pretzels, red wristbands, heart-shaped pins, and new t-shirts. As Marky's classmates were promoted, we expanded Have a Heart Day to include the upper elementary and middle schools. A memorial plaque and a mural of Marky hang prominently just outside of the main front office of BYS, so the students who come behind will know who he was. I am grateful for the tremendous support from the Burlington Township School District. We donated the proceeds to multiple children's hospitals and medical units, the Ronald McDonald House, and the Siani Strong Foundation. Over an eight-year period, we raised over $14,000 for charities that were near and dear to my heart.

Looking back over those years, I realized this annual fundraiser helped to bring healing to me and my family. My family is big on celebrating birthdays. Each family member gets their own day of recognition when we invite family and friends to the house to sing Happy Birthday and eat cake and ice cream. I remember Marky's first birthday party at the McDonald's playground, backyard parties, and even the one when the superhero Batman and the balloon clown showed up to make elaborate balloon creations for the kids. The most memorable birthday party was when Marky's favorite superhero Spider-Man paid him a visit. Spider-Man brought a web full of cheer and wonder to the young children in attendance. Marky's warm, brown eyes lit up with excitement, and his heart was overjoyed. He never knew his Uncle G (my brother George) graciously played the role of Spider-Man. It was a testament to the love George had for his nephew. He dressed up in a costume and portrayed a superhero just to see Marky's smile and make his day.

As I approached Marky's birthday each year, instead of feeling the dread of a birthday without him or the lack of a birthday party, I had a new sense of purpose that fulfilled the longing in my heart. Have a Heart Day became that yearly celebration of Marky's life as we raised money to help other chronically ill children to overcome their challenges and have a better life. I put my time and energy into this project yearly. It was a lot of work but so worth it in the end.

My family members and friends would take off from work and volunteer to sell pretzels all day at the school, along with the school staff members. We looked forward to the camaraderie, seeing Marky's kindergarten teacher, Ms. Nanni, and first-grade teacher, Ms. Leibowitz, and even Ms. Vera Mumford, my grand aunt who worked as an academic achievement aide at BYS for thirty-three years. Aunt Mae, as we affectionately called her, often looked out for Marky and Naomi during the years they attended BYS. At the beginning of the school year, she even took on the afterschool assignment of riding the bus home to ensure students were on the correct buses and returned home safely. She made sure she was assigned to Marky's bus. Aunt Mae would go into Marky's classroom regularly just to check on him. He was always well behaved, paying attention, and doing his best.

I am grateful for all my family, friends, and the Burlington Township School District for supporting this effort and allowing me the space to heal. It was a privilege to be able to follow Marky's classmates throughout their K-12 education. Although I was sad Marky wasn't here to celebrate the many milestones along the way, it brought great joy to my heart to see his classmates thriving. They continued to show their support to us when they invited my husband and me to the class' eighth grade and high school graduations.

This is just one example of the many ways I included others on my journey to healing. I couldn't imagine doing it without the strength and encouragement of my village. I encourage you to find your village and lean in to them to find solace and the heart to move forward.

V— Check Your Vital Signs

When you go to a doctor's visit, the first thing that happens after you get called back to the examination room is the nurse checks your vital signs. They check your weight, body temperature, blood pressure, pulse, and respiration (breathing) rates. All these are considered vital signs because they are measurements of the body's most basic functions. Changes in vital signs or detection of abnormal measurements will alert your health care professional that something may be wrong. Early detection of unfavorable changes in your vital signs is key for timely intervention and improved outcomes.

When you are the primary caretaker of someone who is sick, oftentimes, your health goes unmonitored for long periods of time. Please make the time to go to your own doctor's appointments to ensure your body is getting the attention and treatments needed to have good health and wellness. If your health begins to fail, it will be difficult to provide care for your loved one.

Just as there are physical vital signs to keep in check, there are also other important signs we need to look out for to keep our emotional, mental, and spiritual health in check.

Shortly after Marky's death, my husband and I went to grief counseling at our church. This helped us to recognize the phases of grief that I discussed earlier in Chapter 11. The stages of grief consist of 1) denial, numbness, and shock; 2) bargaining; 3) depression; 4) anger; and 5) acceptance. Grief is the natural healing sequence after we have lost something or someone of great significance. It is painful and doesn't have a specified time limit. According to the article "Grief and Mourning…What's the Difference?", there is a distinction between grief and mourning.[5] Grief consists of the many reactions and emotions you feel after an immense loss. It is the inward expression of loss. Mourning is what you do to adjust to life without your loved one. It is the outward expression of loss, such as visiting a loved one's gravesite, making a scrapbook of your loved one, writing their story, or making a charitable donation in their name.

The important thing for you to know is that you are not alone. Hopefully, you have a trusted friend or relative you can share your feelings with as you move through the stages of grief. Therapy can also be necessary to help guide you through your grief in a healthy manner. There is nothing wrong with seeking counseling for assistance. Let me repeat this. It is okay to seek professional help. Counseling is good for adults as well as children. Even pastors and those in other leadership positions can benefit from therapy too. Pastor Joy Morgan uncovers this revelation in her book *G.E.T. U.P.* She shares how she was surprised when her mentor strongly recommended that she seek therapy after she suffered multiple miscarriages. This had not occurred to her because she was often in the seat of counseling her church members or referring them to seek professional help. However, she later discovered that it was one of the best decisions she could have made. It is therapeutic to talk to someone who has an objective view and who can help guide you through your grief. It can help you discover new things about yourself.

Here are some other techniques I recommend for recovery and healing after a significant loss:

- Get connected or stay connected to your church, a body of believers who share your faith and will encourage you on the journey.
- Attend remembrance ceremonies at the children's hospital.

- Contribute writings to the remembrance journals published by the hospital.
- Attend retreats/conferences to help rebuild your inner man (examples: marriage retreat, women's or men's conference, camps for siblings).

E— Encourage Somebody Else

There is a common saying: In order to have a testimony, you must first go through a test. Share your testimony to inspire others and help them on their journey. You can share the small victories along the way as I did with the online blog. Nowadays, we have social media outlets, which can be an effective platform to share your story. Remember, no matter how bad things are for you, somebody else is going through something far worse. This concept can be applied to other situations, not just when dealing with sickness and death. Find the silver lining of hope in your own situation and hold onto it, and then pass it on to someone else.

Encouragement can come in many forms. I've sat down one on one with grief-stricken women to let them know I feel their pain. I tell them they would eventually get on the other side of this mountain of pain. I send sympathy cards to folks to let them know I am thinking of them. We can certainly send them a quick note of encouragement on social media, but sometimes taking that extra step to personally reach out to them will mean so much more.

I wrote a blog during the time Marky was in the hospital for the last four-and-half months of his life. I initially started the blog to inform our family, friends, and supporters of his medical status and to present our prayer requests. In addition, God was giving me words to write to encourage others through whatever situation they faced. With the help of the Lord, I could look on the bright side and step outside of my own realm of troubles to inspire someone else.

There is a song that the Voices of St. Peter used to sing, originally sung by the legendary gospel songstress Mahalia Jackson. My Grandmom Sylvia would play on the piano, accompanied by Aunt Mae, Aunt Paulette, and my Mother Paula singing the harmonious lyrics, "If I can help somebody, as I pass along… then my living shall not be in vain." I take this message to heart and share my story with the world. I write these pages to leave my son's footprints on the earth, so his legacy of resilience, hope, determination, and strength will be passed on. I hope and pray that this book will encourage others on their journey from grief to healing and wholeness. Then I know my life was not in vain.

Challenge:

1. What are some things you can do to help integrate yourself back into society after a significant loss?

2. In what ways can you apply the principles of L.I.V.E. in your life to regain a new sense of purpose?

Prayer Focus: Dear gracious Father, I am grateful for the different ways You've provided to heal my brokenness. Please walk with me and help me to put the pieces of my life back together so I can live a productive life filled with peace.

CHAPTER 14

Turning Pain into Purpose

Many are the plans in a person's heart,
but it is the Lord's purpose that prevails.
— Proverbs 19:21 (NIV)

As believers in Christ, we know Jesus was crucified on an old rugged cross on the hill of Golgotha. His persecutors were envious of his strength and power and convinced Pilate to order a crucifixion. They mocked Jesus, spit on him, and placed a crown of thorns on his head. Mark 15:21 briefly mentions a man named Simon from Cyrene, a large city in North Africa, who was coming through Jerusalem for the Passover. He heard all the commotion in the courtyard of the governor's headquarters and went to see what was going on. While in the midst of the crowd jeering at the King of the Jews, the soldiers picked Simon out of the boisterous mob and commanded him to carry Jesus' cross for him all the way to Golgotha.

As Simon literally bore the cross for Jesus on that fateful day of his death, each of us has a cross to bear. Marky carried the cross of his illness. He did it most of the time with a smile. When he felt well, he enjoyed life to the fullest, proudly wearing his Spider-Man costume and pretending to web his dad and sister with the secret button on his glove. He rode his bicycle down the street in the cul-de-sac of our neighborhood, feeling free as the wind hit his face. He said please and thank you to his elders, teachers, his friends, and even to the many health care workers he encountered time and time again. He knew the value of time, and he did his best to seize every moment of it and not dwell on the fact that he had a sick heart.

When the Washington family was vacationing in West Virginia one spring, the kids wanted to ride a horse on the ranch. The stable groom picked up three-year-old Marky and placed him on the seat of the saddle on top of the horse. Marky tightly gripped the horn cap with both hands, while his feet were dangling along both sides because they couldn't reach the stirrups. Although he didn't voice it, I could tell he was probably nervous riding on this huge powerful horse. But he faced his fear, put a slight grin on his face and rode that horse around the ring multiple times with the stable groom guiding the way, of course. At that moment, it didn't matter that the doctors said he had a sick heart and probably wouldn't live long. It didn't matter that other surgeries awaited him in the future. He had the opportunity, seized it, and proved that he would have the victorious life even while enduring the sickness.

It was not only the death of my son that we endured, but it was also the death of part of our future with him. I dreamed of seeing him grow up with his sister, graduate high school and college, pursue a career, get married, and have kids of his own. I dreamed of how God would use Marky to share his testimony of healing to those he would encounter from day to day and draw others to Christ. All those dreams were shattered the day he passed away.

I had to come to grips with the fact that my dreams were not in the divine plan of my heavenly Father's. I am reminded of the scripture:

"For my thoughts are not your thoughts, neither are your ways my ways," declares the Lord. As the heavens are higher than the earth, so are my ways higher than your ways and my thoughts than your thoughts."
—Isaiah 55:8-9 (NIV)

Looking back over my life, I can identify three crosses that I bear: dealing with my son's illness, overcoming the grief of his early death, and now broadly sharing the testimony of how God brought me and my family through these difficult times to the place of victory. Like Simon, I did not volunteer to do it. I did not have a choice because I was given these assignments by God. Instead of being angry and wallowing in my sadness, I decided to put my trust in God and have faith that if he gave me the assignments, he would also provide the resources and the strength to accomplish them. My hope and prayer is that in my living out these assignments, I could point others to the God I serve. I pray those who watched me go through these trials could see Christ's character in me. In no way am I saying I am perfect or have it all together. I certainly have my flaws. Nevertheless, I continued to press into what God's Word said and tried to live accordingly so I could experience the fruit of obedience.

There is victory on the other side of your pain. Something good will come out of the trial you are facing. For me, it was having more compassion for those who grieve and empathizing with those who are in the hospital dealing with a chronic condition.

Having a greater appreciation of life helps me to stop and live in the present, enjoy my family time more, and find more reasons to laugh. Our family motto became: Live, Laugh, Love. Those of you who have spent any quality time with me know that I love to take time to enjoy the view, whether it's sliding down the snow-covered slopes of the Pocono Mountains, taking in the scenic views at Coopers Rock State Forest in West Virginia, exploring the nature trails in Maryland, encompassing the red rocks of Sedona, Arizona, or hiking the arduous trail on Sugar Mountain overlooking the Blue Ridge Mountains. There is an inspirational saying, "The best view comes after the hardest climb." I find this to be very true. I can appreciate the trials and struggles I have faced so much more now that I can see them in retrospect.

As I look back over my life, there were many twists and turns I didn't expect. Some caused exhilaration, some anxiety, and sometimes even grief. Losing my son was by far the hardest challenge in my life, but it also gave me the greatest sense of peace because I know it was only God who ordained it, called me to it, and brought me through it. I am here to tell you not only did I survive it, but I can thrive despite my loss. You, too, will survive your loss and you will L.I.V.E. again.

God often has a purpose for the trouble He allows into our lives. With his help, we can find the balance between planning our future and responding to the adversities of life that will come. When we submit our aspirations and dreams to God, then He'll show us what he wants to accomplish in us and through us. My prayer is for each of you to have the Heart to Move Forward and L.I.V.E. Again.

CHALLENGE:

1. What cross are you bearing? What assignment has God given to you to complete? If you don't know, ask someone you trust who knows your story and can give you an objective view of what they see in you.

2. Are you willing to embrace your assignment? What steps can you take to fulfill this assignment?

3. What have you learned about yourself during your journey?

Prayer Focus: Loving God, help me to fulfill the purpose You've given to me. Show me the assignment(s) and how to complete it so You get the glory and the honor. Surround me with the people and resources I need to accomplish it. Thank You, Lord, for giving me purpose.

CHAPTER 15

SAVE A LIFE

After this extraordinary journey with Marky, I realized the importance of organ donation. My husband and I registered to become organ donors through our state, and this is officially noted on our driver's license. I was thinking to myself, what else can I do to help other patients who are waiting for a life-saving organ? I can spread the word about the need for people to register to be tissue and organ donors. Here are some important facts to know about organ donation and transplantation.

There are seven reasons why one should consider becoming an organ donor:[6]

1. As of February 2021, there are more than 107,000 people on the transplant list waiting for an organ.

2. Only 39,000 transplants were performed in 2020.

3. Seventeen people die each day waiting for an organ transplant.

4. Ninety percent of U.S. adults support organ donation, but only sixty percent are actually signed up as donors.

5. Every nine minutes, another person is added to the transplant waiting list.

6. Only three in 1,000 people die in a way that allows for organ donation.

7. One donor can save eight lives. One person can donate up to eight lifesaving organs. {heart, two lungs, liver, pancreas, two kidneys, intestines}

You could possibly save up to eight lives by making the important decision to become an organ donor. It is an easy registration process. Go to www.organdonor.gov to read the information on what tissue and organ donation is and how to sign up at the state level.

The Myths of Organ Donation

There are many myths that scare people away from becoming organ donors. Get the facts first before making a decision. Here are just a few of the myths and the facts that correspond:

1. **Myth:** If they see I'm a donor at the hospital, they won't try to save my life.[7] **Fact:** When you are sick or injured and admitted to the hospital, the one and only priority is to save your life. Donation doesn't become a possibility until all lifesaving methods have failed.

2. **Myth:** I'm too old to be a donor. **Fact:** There's no age limit to organ donation. The oldest donor in the U.S. was age ninety-three. As long as the organs are in good health and condition, they can be donated.

3. **Myth:** I have a medical condition, so I can't be a donor. **Fact:** Anyone, regardless of age or medical history, can sign up to be a donor. The transplant team will determine if the organs or tissues can be donated.

4. **Myth:** My family won't be able to have an open casket funeral if I'm a donor. **Fact:** An open casket funeral is usually possible for organ, eye, and tissue donors.

Take the time to educate yourself on the benefits of organ donation. There needs to be a more diverse pool of organ donations so those who are on the long waiting lists will have a better chance of getting matching organs. Please consider saving a life. It can be your last opportunity to help somebody else on this earth as you transition to your eternal destination.

If you decide to become an organ donor after reading my story or hearing me speak about this topic, please feel free to go to my website dynitawashington.com to let me know. I would love to hear how this message impacted your decision.

May the Lord bless you and your family as you travel on your own journey. Check out the Resources page to find a list of websites with good information to support you as you manage life with a sick child or as you are processing the death of a loved one. I pray this book has been a blessing to you and will propel you to L.I.V.E.

About the Author

Dynita Tanya Sills Washington grew up in Burlington, New Jersey. She earned several scholarships and was afforded the opportunity to attend the University of Pennsylvania in West Philadelphia.

Her skill with numbers and love of young people led her to graduate from Penn with a Bachelor of Arts Degree in Mathematics and a Master of Science Degree in Higher Education Administration. She married the love of her life, Mark Washington in 1996. They settled down in South Jersey and later had two children and two foster children.

After the death of Dynita's first born son in 2007, she co-founded the "Have A Heart Day" fundraiser to support chronically ill children and their families. Dynita currently lives in Baltimore, Maryland with her husband, Mark, of twenty-four years and their daughter, Naomi. Her career in higher education continues at Johns Hopkins University where she has worked for the last four years. She is active in the Worship and Arts, Women's, and Marriage Ministries at Bridgeway Community Church in Columbia, Maryland.

Dynita has served in the music ministry since she was a little girl. She is a strong woman of faith who has faced many adversities. With each trial she has learned to stand on the Word of God and declare victory over her life. With her inaugural book, she turns her pain into purpose as she encourages other parents to move past their struggles towards a life of victory.

Visit her online at DynitaWashington.com.

Resources

Websites

American Association for Marriage and Family Therapy: https://aamft.org/ - Use the AAMFT portal to find a trained therapist for family and marriages in your area.

Bereaved Parents of the U.S.A.: www.bereavedparentsusa.org - A self-help group that offers support, understanding, compassion and hope to bereaved parents, grandparents and siblings.

Birth Injury Guide: https://www.birthinjuryguide.org/ - Provides free legal consultation and to get information about compensation that may be available for birth injuries or medical malpractice.

Candlelighters Childhood Cancer Foundation: www.candlelighters.org - Founded by parents of children with cancer, this group offers support to parents who have a child diagnosed with cancer and those whose child has died of cancer.

CaringBridge: https://www.caringbridge.org/ - A resource to create your personal blog; to build bridges of care and communication providing love and support on a health journey.

To visit the blog for Marky Washington go to: https://www.caringbridge.org/visit/markywashington - You can select your own login and password to access the site. You can visit the photo gallery and read the journal entries.

Compassionate Friends: www.compassionatefriends.org - An organization for bereaved parents, assisting families following the death of a child.

First Candle/SIDS Alliance: firstcandle.org - Support for families who have experienced miscarriage, stillbirth or sudden death of an infant.

Grief and Mourning: griefandmourning.com - A website with a blog, articles, private online group sessions for those who are grieving.

Grief Share Program: griefshare.org - An organization with a friendly, caring group of people who will walk alongside you through one of life's most difficult experiences.

Health Resources & Services Administration—Organ Donation and Transplantation: https://www.organdonor.gov/ - U.S. federal entity that provides information about the need for organ and tissue donations, the process of organ transplantation, and how to register in your state.

Mothers Against Drunk Driving (MADD): https://www.madd.org - The mission of MADD is to end drunk driving, help fight drugged driving, support the victims of these violent crimes, and prevent underage drinking.

National Center for Missing and Exploited Children: https://www.missingkids.org/ - The nation's nonprofit clearinghouse and comprehensive reporting center for all issues related to the prevention of and recovery from child victimization.

The National Hospice and Palliative Care Organization: https://www.nhpco.org/ - An organization representing palliative care and hospice programs and professionals in the U.S., committed to improving end-of-life care and increasing access to hospice care.

National Organization of Parents of Murdered Children: https://pomc.org/ - For the families and friends of those who have died by violence.

Ronald McDonald House: www.rmhc.org - Support for families around the world while sick children receive medical treatment at the hospital.

The Ulman House: https://ulmanfoundation.org/ulman-house/ - Changing lives by creating a community of support for young adults, and their loved ones, impacted by cancer. Provides temporary housing and meals for young adults receiving cancer treatments at local hospitals in Baltimore, MD.

Books Mentioned

1. Morgan, Joy. *G.E.T. U.P.: 5 Steps to Bouncing Back When Life Knocks You Down*. Burlington: MYJOY Publishing, 2016. Kindle.

2. Roberts, Liardon. *We Saw Heaven: True Stories of What Awaits Us on the Other Side.* Shippensburg. Destiny Image Publishers, 2000.

WORKS CITED

1., 2. "Congenital Heart Defects," Centers for Disease Control and Prevention, last reviewed December 9, 2020 https://www.cdc.gov/ncbddd/heartdefects/data.html.

3. Hendriksen, Ellen. "Should Moms Work or Stay at Home?" Savvy Psychologist. June 12, 2015. https://www.quickanddirtytips.com/health-fitness/mental-health/should-moms-work-or-stay-at-home.

4. Doggett, Jolie A. "9 Things Foster Parents Want You to Know About the Foster Care System." Huff Post. May, 23, 2019. https://www.huffpost.com/entry/need-to-know-about-foster-parent_l_5ce5526ae4b0d513447dc00e

5. "Grief and Mourning…What's the Difference?" https://griefandmourning.com/

6. Health Resources and Services Administration. "Organ Donation Statistics." Assessed June 9, 2021. https://www.organdonor.gov/statistics-stories/statistics.html

7. Health Resources and Services Administration. "Organ Donation Myths and Facts."Assessed June 9, 2021. https://www.organdonor.gov/about/facts-terms/donation-myths-facts.html

Connect

If you enjoyed this book, please purchase copies for your loved ones, and leave a review on Amazon.com. To order additional or bulk copies, visit dynitawashington.com/

Contact the Author:

Dynita Washington Enterprises

Email: dynitawashingtonenterprises@outlook.com

Website: dynitawashington.com

Facebook: https://www.facebook.com/dynita.sillswashington

Instagram: https://www.instagram.com/dynitawashington/

Made in the USA
Las Vegas, NV
21 July 2021